THE

Constitution and Laws

OF THE

OSAGE NATION,

PASSED AT

PAWHUSKA, OSAGE NATION,

In the Years 1881 and 1882.

CONSTITUTION AND LAWS

OF THE

SAC AND FOX NATION

INDIAN TERRITORY.

The Constitution of the Sac and Fox Nation, Prepared by the Authorized Committee, and Adopted by the National Council.

SR Scholarly Resources Inc.
Wilmington, Delaware

SCHOLARLY RESOURCES, INC.
Wilmington, Delaware

Reprint edition published in 1975

Library of Congress Catalog Card Number: 75-3699
ISBN: 0-8420-1891-3

Manufactured in the United States of America

THE

Constitution and Laws

OF THE

OSAGE NATION,

PASSED AT

PAWHUSKA, OSAGE NATION,

In the Years 1881 and 1882.

[illegible]

[illegible]

[illegible]

CONSTITUTION

OF

THE OSAGE NATION.

The Constitution of the Osage Nation, prepared by the authorized committee and adopted by the National Council.

The Great and Little Osages having united and become one body politic, under the style and title of the Osage Nation; therefore,

We, the people of the Osage Nation, in National Council assembled, in order to establish justice, insure tranquility, promote the common welfare, and to secure to ourselves and our posterity the blessing of freedom—acknowledging with humility and gratitude the goodness of the Sovereign Ruler of the universe in permitting us so to do, and imploring his aid and guidance in its accomplishment—do ordain and establish this Constitution for the government of the Osage Nation.

ARTICLE I.

SECTION 1. The boundary of the Osage Nation shall be that described in the treaty of 1876 between the United States and the Great and Little Osages, except that portion purchased by the Kaws.

SEC. 2. The lands of the Osage Nation shall remain common property, until the National Council shall request an allotment of the same, but the improvements made thereon and in possession of the citizens of this Nation are the exclusive and indefeasible property of the citizens respectively who made or may rightfully be in possession of them. *Provided*, That the citizen of this Nation possessing exclusive and indeasible right to their improvements, as expressed in this article, shall possess no right or power to dispose of their improvements in any manner whatever, to the United States, individual States, or to individual citizens thereof; and that, whenever any citizen shall remove with his effects out of the limits of this Nation, and become a citizen of any other government, all his rights and privileges as a citizen of this Nation shall cease; *Provided, nevertheless*, That the National Council shall have power to re-admit by law, to all the rights of citizenship any such persons who may at any time desire to return to the Nation, on memorializing the National Council for such readmission.

Moreover, the National Council shall have power to adopt such laws and regulations as it may deem expedient and proper to prevent citizens from monopolizing improvements with the view of speculation.

ARTICLE II.

SECTION 1. The power of this government shall be divided into three distinct departments, the Legislative, the Executive, and the Judicial.

SEC. 2. No person or persons belonging to one of these departments shall exercise any of the powers properly belonging to either of the others, except in the cases hereinafter expressly directed or permitted.

ARTICLE III.

SECTION 1. The legislative power shall be vested in a National Council, and the style of their acts shall be:—Be it enacted by the National Council.

SEC. 2. The National Council shall make provision, by law, for laying off the Osage Nation into five districts, and, if subsequently it should be deemed expedient, one or two may be added thereto.

SEC. 3. The National Council shall consist of three members from each district, to be chosen by the qualified electors in their respective district, for two years, the elections to be held in the respective districts every two years, at such times and places as may be directed by law,

The National Council shall, after the present year, be held annually, to be convened on the first Monday in November, at such place as may be designated by the National Council, or, in case of emergency, by the Principal Chief.

SEC. 4. Before the districts shall be laid off, any election which may take place, shall be by general vote of the electors throughout the Nation, for all officers to be elected.

The first election for all officers of the government.—Chiefs, Executive Council, members of the National Council, Judges, and Sheriffs—shall be held at Pawhuska, before the rising of this council; and the term of service of all officers elected previous to the first Monday in November, 1882, shall be extended to embrace, in addition to the regular constitutional term, the time intervening from their election to the first Monday in November, 1882.

SEC. 5. No person shall be eligible to a seat in the National Council, but an Osage male citizen, who shall have attained to the age of twenty-five years.

SEC. 6. The members of the National Council shall in all cases, except those of felony or breach of the peace, be privileged from arrest during their attendance at the National Council, in going to, and returning.

SEC. 7. In all elections by the people the electors shall vote *viva voce*. All male citizens, who shall have attained to the age of eighteen years, shall be equally entitled to vote at all public elections.

SEC. 8. The National Council shall judge of the qualifications and returns of its own members, determine the rules of its proceedings, punish a member for disorderly behavior, and with the concurrence of two-third, expel a member; but not a second time for the same offence.

SEC. 9. The National Council, when assembled, shall chose its own officers; a majority shall constitute a quorum to do business, but a smaller number may adjourn from day to day and compel the attendance of absent members, in such manner, and under such penalty as the council may prescribe.

SEC. 10. The members of the National Council shall each receive a compensation for their services, which shall be one hundred dollars per annum: *Provided*, That the same may be increased or diminished by law; but no alteration shall take effect during the period of services of the members of the National Council by whom such alteration may have been made.

SEC. 11. The National Council shall regulate by law, by whom, and in what manner, writs of elections shall be issued to fill the vacancies which may happen in the Council thereof.

SEC. 12. Each member of the National Council, before he takes his seat, shall take the following oath or affirmation:

"I, A. B., do solemnly swear (or affirm, as the case may be) that I have not obtained my election by bribery, treat, or any undue and unlawful means, used by myself, or others, by my desire or approbation for that purpose; that I consider myself constitutionally qualified as a member of————, and that on all questions and measures which may come before me, I will so give my vote, and so conduct myself, as, in my judgment, shall appear most conducive to the interest and prosperity of this Nation, and that I will bear true faith and allegiance to the same, and to the utmost of my ability and power, observe, conform to, support, and defend the constitution thereof."

SEC. 13. No person who may be convicted of felony shall

be eligible to any office or appointment of honor, profit or trust, within this Nation.

SEC. 14. The National Council shall have power to make all laws and regulations which they shall deem necessary and proper for the good of the Nation, which shall not be contrary to this constitution.

SEC. 15. It shall be the duty of the National Council to pass such laws as may be necessary and proper to decide differences by arbitration, to be appointed by the parties who may choose that summary mode of adjustment.

SEC. 16. No power of suspending the laws of this Nation shall be exercised, unless by the National Council or its authority.

SEC. 17. No retrospective law, nor any law impairing the obligations of contracts, shall be passed.

SEC. 18. The National Council shall have power to make laws for laying and collecting taxes for the purpose of raising a revenue.

SEC. 19. All acknowledged treaties shall be the supreme law of the land, and the National Council shall have the sole power of deciding on the constructions of all treaty stipulations.

SEC. 20. The Council shall have the sole power of impeaching. All impeachments shall be tried by the National Council, when setting for that purpose; the members shall be upon oath or affirmation; and no person shall be convicted without the concurrence of two-thirds of the members present.

SEC. 21. The Principal Chief, Assistant Principal Chief, and all civil officers shall be liable to impeachment for misdemeanor in office; but judgment in such cases shall not extend further than removal from office, and disqualification to hold any office of honor, trust, or profit under the government of this Nation. The party, whether convicted or acquitted, shall, nevertheless, be liable to indictment, trial, judgment, and punishment according to law.

ARTICLE IV.

SECTION 1. The supreme executive power of this Nation shall be vested in a Principal Chief, who shall be styled "The Principal Chief of the Osage Nation." The Principal Chief shall hold his office for the term of two years, and shall be elected by the qualified electors on the same day, and at the place where they shall respectively vote for members to the National Council. The returns of the elections for Principal Chief shall be sealed up and directed to the President of the National Council, who shall open and publish them in the presence of the Council assembled. The person having the highest number of votes shall be Principal Chief, but if two or more shall be equal and highest in votes, one of them shall be chosen by vote of the National Council; the manner of determining contested elections shall be directed by law.

SEC. 2. No person, except a natural born citizen, shall be eligible to the office of Principal Chief; neither shall any person be eligible to that office who shall not have attained to the age of thirty-five years.

SEC. 3. There shall also be chosen, at the same time, by the qualified electors, in the same manner, for two years, an Assistant Principal Chief, who shall have attained to the age of thirty-five years.

SEC. 4. In case of the removal of the Principal Chief from office, or of his death, or resignation, or inability to discharge the powers and duties of the said office, the same shall devolve on the Assistant Principal Chief.

SEC. 5. The National Council may, by law, provide for the case of removal, death, resignation, or disability of both the Principal and Assistant Principal Chief, declaring what officer shall then act as Principal Chief until the disability be removed or a Principal Chief shall be elected.

SEC. 6. The Principal Chief and Assistant Principal Chief shall, at stated times, receive for their services a compensation which shall neither be increased nor diminished during the period for which they shall have been elected, and they shall not receive within that period any other emolument from the Osage Nation or any other government."

SEC. 7. Before the Principal Chief enters on the execution of his office, he shall take the following oath or affirmation: "I do solemnly swear or affirm that I will faithfully execute the duties of Principal Chief of the Osage Nation, and will, to the best of my ability, preserve, protect, and defend the Constitution of the Osage Nation.

SEC. 8. He may, on extraordinary occasions, convene the National Council at the seat of government.

SEC. 9. He shall, from time to time, give to the Council information of the state of the government, and recommend to their consideration such measures as he may deem expedient.

SEC. 10. He shall take care that the laws be faithfully executed.

SEC. 11. It shall be his duty to visit the different districts at least once in two years, to inform himself of the general condition of the country.

SEC. 12. The Assistant Principal Chief shall, by virtue of his office, aid and advise the Principal Chief in the administration of the government at all times during his continuance in office.

SEC. 13. Vacancies that may occur in offices, the appointment of which is vested in the National Council shall be filled by the Principal Chief during the recess of the National Council, by granting commissions, which shall expire at the end of the next session thereof.

SEC. 14. Every bill, which shall pass the National Council, shall, before it becomes a law, be presented to the Principal Chief; if he approves, he shall sign it, but if not, he shall return it with his objections to the Council, who shall enter the objections at large on their journals, and proceed to reconsider it.

If, after such reconsideration, two-thirds of the Council shall agree to pass the bill, it become a law, if any bill shall not be returned by the Principal Chief within five days (Sunday excepted) after the same has been presented to him, it shall become law, in like manner as if he had signed it. Unless the National Council, by their adjournment, prevent its return, in which case it shall be a law, unless sent back within three days after their next meeting.

SEC. 15. Members of the National Council and all officers, executive and judicial, shall be bound by oath, to support the Constitution of their Nation; and to perform the duties of their respective offices with fidelity.

SEC. 16. The Principal Chief shall, during the session of the National Council, attend at the seat of government.

SEC. 17. The Principal Chief shall recommend three persons, to be appointed by the National Council, whom the Principal Chief shall have full power at his discretion to assemble; he, together with the Assistant Principal Chief and the Counsellors, or a majority of them, may, from time to time, hold and keep a Council for ordering and directing the affairs of the Nation according to law.

SEC. 18. The members of the Executive Council shall be chosen for the term of two years.

SEC. 19. The Treasurer of the Osage Nation shall be chosen by the National Council for the term of two years.

SEC. 20. The Treasurer shall, before entering on the duties of his office, give bond to the Nation with Sureties to the satisfaction of the National Council, for the faithful discharge of his trust.

SEC. 21. No money shall be drawn from the treasury, but by warrant from the Principal Chief, and in consequence of appropriations made by law.

SEC. 22. It shall be the duty of the Treasurer to receive all public moneys, and to make a regular statement and account of the receipts and expenditures of all public moneys at the annual session of the National Council.

SEC. 23. The "Fiscal Year" of the Osage Nation shall begin on the 1st day of October, and close on the 30th day of September of each year; and all books and accounts of the Treasurer, shall be kept, and duties of his office performed with regard to the beginning and ending of the fiscal year, The National Treasurer shall receive for his services ten (10) per cent. of all moneys that may pass through his hands as provided by law.

ARTICLE V.

SECTION 1. The judicial powers shall be vested in a supreme court, and such circuits and inferior courts as the National Council may from time to time ordain and establish.

SEC. 2. The judges of the supreme and circuits courts shall hold their commission for the term of two years, but any of them may be removed from office on the address of two-thirds of the National Council to the Principal Chief, for that purpose.

SEC. 3. The judges of the supreme court and circuits courts, shall at stated times receive a compensation which shall not be deminished during their continuance in office, but they shall receive no fees or perquisites of office, nor hold any other office of profit or trust under the government of this Nation or any other power.

SEC. 4. No person shall be appointed a judge of any of the courts, until he shall have attained the age of thirty years.

SEC. 5. The judges of the Supreme and Circuits courts shall be elected by the National Council.

SEC. 6. The judges of the Supreme courts and of the Circuits courts shall have complete criminal jurisdiction in such cases and in such manner as may be pointed out by law.

SEC. 7. No judge shall sit on trial of any cause when the parties are connected (with him) by affinity or consanguinity except by consent of the parties. In case all the judges of the supreme court shall be interested in the issue of any court or related to all or either of the parties, the National Council may provide by law for the selection of a suitable number of persons of good character and knowledge for the determination thereof, and who shall be specially commissioned for the adjudication of such case by the Principal Chief.

SEC. 8. All writs and other process shall run "in the name of the Osage Nation" and bear test and be signed by the respective clerks.

SEC. 9. Indictments shall conclude against the peace and dignity of the Osage Nation.

SEC. 10. The supreme court shall, after the present year, hold its session three times a year, at the seat of government, to be convened on the first Monday in October, February, and August, of each year.

SEC. 11. In all criminal prosecutions the accused shall have the right of being heard; of demanding the nature of the accusation; of meeting the witnesses face to face; of having compulsory process for obtaining witnesses in his or their favor, and in prosecutions by indictment or information a speedy public trial; nor shall the accused be compelled to give evidence against himself.

SEC. 12. All persons shall be bailable by sufficient securities, unless for capital offences when the proof is evident or presumption great.

ARTICLE VI.

SECTION 1. No person who denies the being of a God or a future state of reward and punishment, shall hold any office in the civil department in this Nation.

SEC. 2. When the National Council shall determine the expediency of appointing delegates, or other public agents for the purpose of transacting business with the Government of the United States, the Principal Chief shall recommend, and by the advice and consent of the National Council appoint and commission such delegates or public agents accordingly on all matters of interest touching the rights of the citizens of this Nation which may require the attention of the United States Government.

SEC 3. All commissions shall be in the name and by the authority of the Osage Nation, and signed by the Principal Chief. The Principal Chief shall make use of his private seal until a national one shall be provided.

SEC. 4. A sheriff shall be elected in each district by the qualified electors thereof, who shall hold his office two years unless sooner removed. Should a vacancy occur subsequent to election, it shall be filled by the Principal Chief as in other cases, and the person so appointed shall continue in office until the next regular election.

SEC. 5. The appointment of all officers not otherwise directed by this constitution shall be for voted in the National Council.

SEC. 6. The National Council may propose such amendments to this Constitution as two-thirds of the Council may deem expedient, and the Principal Chief shall issue a proclamation directing all officers of the several districts to promulgate the same as extensively as possible within their respective districts at least six months previous to the next general election, and if, at the first session of council after such general election, two-thirds of the council shall by ayes and noes ratify such proposed amendments, they shall be valid to all extent and purposes as part of this Constitution, *Provided*, that such proposed amendments shall be read on three several days in Council, as well as when the same are proposed as when they are ratified.

Done in convention at Pawhuska, Osage Nation, this thirty-first day of December, A. D. 1881.

JAMES BIGHEART,
President of the National Cenvention
Ne-kah-ke-pon-ah.
Wah-ti-an-kah.
Saucy Chief.
Tah-wah-che-he.
William Penn.
Clamore.
Two-giver.
Tall-chief.
Sa-pah-ke-ah.
Black Dog.
Thomas Big-chief.
Ne-kah-wah-she-ton-kah.
Joseph Pawnee-no-pah she
White Hair.
Cyprian Tayrian.

PAUL AKIN, *Interpreter.*
E. M. MATTHEWS,
Secretary.

LAWS

OF

THE OSAGE NATION.

CHAPTER 2.

ARTICLE I.

An Act for the punishment of criminal offences.

SECTION 1. That in all cases of wilful murder, the offender, upon trial and conviction by the authorized court of this Nation, shall suffer death, and when sentence of death shall have been passed, the court shall grant a respite of five days before such criminal shall be executed.

SEC. 2. That any person who shall, with malice aforethought, assault another with intent to kill, shall, upon conviction thereof, be fined in a sum, for the benefit of the party injured, not less than fifty nor more than one hundred dollars, at the discretion of the court, and receive fifty lashes on the bare back. But if any person shall kill in self-defence or by accident, without any previous intent to do the same, he shall not be held accountable for such act, and be exempt from any fine or punishment whatever.

SEC. 3. That upon trial and conviction of any person charged with the offence of having committed a rape on any female, he shall be punished with fifty lashes on the bare back.

ARTICLE 2.

An Act for the punishment of thefts and other crime.

SEC. 4. That any person who shall be convicted of stealing a horse, mule, jack or jinney, shall be punished by not less than twenty-nine nor more than fifty lashes on the bare back, and be compelled to make payment to the amount of damages or injuries sustained, if such stolen property be not restored, for the benefit of the person so injured; and for all other property which may be stolen, upon conviction of the party so offending, the punishment shall be in proportion to the magnitude of the offence, at the discretion of the court, and judgment against the offender for damages to the party injured.

SEC. 5. That if any person shall wilfully and maliciously burn the house or other property of another, or otherwise kill or destroy the property of any person for the purpose of injuring or gratifying a spirit of revenge, such offender, upon conviction, shall be punished in like manner as provided in the section above, and be compelled to make ample remuneration by such compensation as the Court may determine.

SEC. 6. That any person who shall employ another, or aid or abet in the perpetration of any criminal offence, upon conviction thereof, such person or persons shall suffer such punishment as may be inflicted upon the principal offender; and be likewise subject to the same judgment for damages.

ARTICLE III.

AN ACT *in relation to contracts.*

SEC. 7. That all lawful contracts shall be binding, and any person upon failure to comply with the terms of such contracts shall be liable to a suit at law, in the Court having jurisdiction in the matter, to be instituted by the creditor, and if upon trial, the law and testimony shall justify judgment shall be rendered in favor of such creditor for the amount which may be due by the defendant.

SEC. 8. That in all cases where a debt may be contracted, and it is agreed that property or trade shall be taken in payment of such debt, judgment shall be rendered accordingly; and the officer shall proceed to levy on the property of such debtor, and to summons two disinterested citizens, who shall be sworn by him, to aid in the valuation of such property, fairly and impartially, and when such property is so valued by the sheriff and such other persons, the creditor shall receive the same at such valuation as may be fixed by them.

SEC. 9. The following description of property shall be exempt from sale to satisfy any debt or judgment, and shall be reserved for the benefit of the owner thereof; viz: one horse or in lieu thereof, one yoke of oxen, one cow and calf, one sow and pigs, farming utensils, household and kitchen furniture, and fifty bushels of corn, and fire-arms, one saddle and bridle, and it shall not be lawful for an officer to levy on any of the above-mentioned property.

SEC. 10. When judgment is rendered, and the officer in whose hands an execution may be placed shall fail to find any property or effects in possession of the debtor to satisfy the same, and has cause to believe that some other person has in hands property or effects belonging to such debtor, the officer shall proceed to make inquiry of such person; and if such property or effects shall be pointed out, he shall proceed to make levy; but if such person shall refuse to give such information as may be satisfactory, the officer shall summon him before the clerk of the court, who shall require of him an oath to answer to the charges of holding in his possession the property or effects of such debtor.

SEC. 11. It shall not be lawful for any officer to levy on

the house, farm, or any other improvements, of any person or persons.

ARTICLE IV.

AN ACT *respecting persons who may be summoned by an officer.*

SEC. 12. Any person or persons who may be summoned to appear before the court to give in testimony, and shall refuse or fail to attend, unless on account of sickness or other lawful excuse—such person shall be fined in a sum not less than twenty, nor more than fifty dollars, at the discretion of the court; and any person who may be summoned by an officer to aid in the arrest of any criminal, and shall refuse, unless it shall be on account of sickness, or other lawful excuse, shall be fined twenty-five dollars.

SEC. 13. Any citizen who may be summoned to assist in arresting criminals shall be entitled to one dollar per day for his services out of the national treasury; and all persons summoned to give in testimony in court shall be entitled each to one dollar per day during their attendance at court, including going and returning home—against whom judgment may be rendered.

ARTICLE V.

AN ACT *relating to estates and administrators.*

SEC. 14. All written or verbal wills of deceased persons, when proved to the satisfaction of one of the judges of the court, shall be valid, and if by such will, any person or persons are designated to manage the business of any estate so left, such person shall receive from one of the judges of the court a written appointment for that purpose, and be required to enter into bond with sufficient security, for the faithful management of such business, in accordance with the provisions of said will, and for the careful preservation of all property and effects so left, all such wills shall be registered by the clerk of the court. All persons so appointed shall furnish, on oath, a schedule and discription of all property and effects belonging to such estate, and which shall likewise be registered by the said clerk.

SEC. 15. Executors of wills and administrators on estate of deceased persons shall report annually to the judges of the court at the August term of the Supreme Court, the condition of, and all that may have been done by them in reference to the business, property, and effects of such estate, as such persons may have in charge.

SEC. 16. Executors of wills and administrators shall be entitled to a compensation of eight per cent. upon the amount of property and effects belonging to an estate, for their services, which shall be appraised by two or more persons to be appointed by the Chief Justice under oath.

SEC. 17. When a person dies without having made a will, one of the judges shall grant letters of administration to some competent and responsible person, to be selected from among the relatives of the deceased, if the safety of such property as may be left seems to warrant, and who shall be required to enter into bond, as provided above. And the property and effects shall belong equally to the children; the widow, also, of such deceased person shall be entitled to an equal share with the children, to be apportioned to her whenever she requires it, and the settlement of the business will safely permit, and the residue to the children as they become of age, to wit, males at eigh. .n years, and females at fifteen years, and in case such widow shall again marry and hold her property separately from her husband, and shall die without issue from her second marriage, such property shall be divided among the aforesaid children, and in all cases where the wife dies holding property as above, and has children, and the husband survives, such property shall likewise be equally apportioned among the children and the husband; and if such husband should again marry and die without issue from such second marriage, his property shall be divided equally among his children. Any administrator, who may have charge of an estate, shall settle all just debts due out of its effects, and collect all outstanding claims in its favor. He shall cause public notice to be given, by written advertisements, for all persons having demands against such es*ate to bring them forward for settlement within twelve months, otherwise they shall be void and not recoverable by law.

ARTICLE VI.

An Act relating to Public Domain.

SEC. 18. No person or persons shall be permitted to settle on or erect any improvements within one-fourth of a mile of the house, field or other improvements of another citizen, without their consent, under the penalty of forfeiting such improvements and labor for the benefit of the original settler; provided it may be lawful, however, where there may be a stream of running water for another citizen to improve one hundred yards from such field so situated.

SEC. 19. All improvements which may be left by any person or persons removing to another place, and the improvements so left remaining unoccupied for the term of two years, such improvements shall be considered abandoned, and other person or persons whosoever may take and go in possession of such improvements in the same manner as if there were no improvements.

ARTICLE VII.

An Act to legalize intermarriage with white men.

SEC. 20. Whereas the peace and prosperity of the Osage people require that, in the enforcement of the laws, jurisdiction of the civil laws should be exercised over all persons whatever, who may, from time to time, be privileged to reside within the limits of the Osage Nation; therefore, any white man or citizen of the United States, who may hereafter come into the country to marry an Osage woman, shall first be required to make known his intentions to the National Council by applying for a license, and such license may, under the authority of the National Council, be issued by the clerk thereof; any person so obtaining a license shall pay to the clerk the sum of twenty dollars for such license, and take an oath to support the Constitution and abide by the laws of the Osage Nation; which oath may be administered by the President of the National Council, or the Clerk of the body, authorized for that purpose, and it shall be the duty of the Clerk to record the same in the Journals of the National Council. But if any such white man, or citizen of the United States, shall refuse to ubscribe to the oath, he shall not be entitled to the rights of citizenship, and shall forthwith be removed without the limits of the Osage Nation as an intruder.

ARTICLE VIII.

An Act respecting stray property.

SEC. 21. It shall be the duty of each of the sheriffs of the several districts to receive and advertise for public sale to the highest bidder all stray property that may be found or reported to them in their respective districts—such as horses, mules, asses, cows, hogs, sheep, and goats—giving a description of color, brands, ear and flesh marks, age and sex, and such property shall be sold for prompt payment in cash, national warrants, or certificates, at the regular term of court, and on the first day thereof, and not before the hour of ten in the morning.

SEC. 22. All stray property, before being sold, shall be advertised at least sixty days by written advertisements, and posted at the court-house, and in like manner in the register-book, which shall be kept by the clerk of the court;

and any person having property advertised under the provision of this act shall have the right of reclaiming such property by providing the same, on or before the day of sale, before one of the judges of the court; and the judge, if satisfied of the proof, after recording the same, and making his decision thereon, shall issue an order directing the sheriff posting the property to deliver it to the owner.

SEC. 23. If any person having property advertised under this act shall fail to prove the same, before the sale of the same, he shall forfeit his right to such property, except as hereinafter provided; but any person who shall prove such property in the manner thereinbefore provided for, within nine months after the sale of the same, shall be entitled to receive from the Treasurer, on the certificate of the judge before whom the proof is made, the proceeds in kind of the sale of the same, deducting therefrom the sheriff's fees.

SEC. 24. Any person who may take up stray property shall, within ten days thereafter, be required to have the same posted; and any person failing to comply with this provision shall be liable to a fine of not less than ten nor more than twenty-five dollars.

SEC. 25. Any person who shall dispose of or wilfully take any stray property not his own, or shall wilfully kill or maim any such property, either before or after such property is posted, shall be deemed guilty of the same offence as if the act was committed upon the property of a citizen, and shall, upon conviction, be punished accordingly.

SEC. 26. It shall be the duty of the several sheriffs to have, if possible, all property that may be posted by them at the Court-house on the day of sale, and to place the purchaser there in possession of the same when sold, or within a reasonable time, if required to do so; the sheriff may retain ten per cent. in kind of all proceeds of sales of stray property, and be required to turn over the residue to the treasurer. The clerk of the court shall be present at all sales of stray property, and shall make and keep on record in his office a register of all sales by the sheriff, to whom made, amount in kind paid, date of sale and kind of property sold, and make therefrom a quarterly report to treasurer as he may direct.

ARTICLE IX.

AN ACT *relating to the duties of the High Sheriff.*

SEC. 27. The office of High Sheriff is hereby created. He shall be elected by the National Council for the term of two years.

SEC. 28. It shall be the duty of the High Sheriff to keep the Capitol, the furniture, and other property therein and thereto belonging in a State, of the keys and fastening of the door of the Capitol during the session of the National Council and the sitting of the Court.

SEC. 29. The Sheriff shall at all times keep the room of the Capitol clean and properly ventilated, and during the session of the National Council and Court well-warmed and supplied with pure water. It shall be his especial duty to cause to be prosecuted every person who shall be accused of violating the laws.

SEC. 30. The High Sheriff shall be a conservator of the peace with such general powers as are exercised by Sheriffs, besides such special or extraordinary powers as may be conferred upon him by law. He shall wait upon, open and adjourn the session of the Court and execute its mandates. He shall also wait upon and execute all orders of the National Council we shall have full authority during the session of the Council, and at all other times to suppress within the vicinity of the Capital all riotous broils, obscene, or other improper conduct, and to enforce obedience to the law and may, whenever necessary, summons any extra adequate force to his assistance; he may summarily arrest, imprison, and hold untilduly sober, any person acting improperly, while under the influence of intoxicating drinks, and arrest, and imprison, all persons who may be guilty of a breach of the peace at or about the same of government.

SEC. 31. The High Sheriff shall have general supervision of the lower sheriffs, and see that they properly execute the laws in their respective districts, and he shall see that all taxes are collected as provided by law.

ARTICLE X.

Duties of the Prosecuting Attorney.

SEC. 32. The Prosecuting Attorney shall be elected at the same time and in the manner that executive councilors are elected, and his term of office shall be that of the National Council electing him, and such prosecuting attorney before he enters upon the duties of his office shall be commissioned by the principal chief, his compensation shall be two hundred dollars per annum.

SEC. 33. That it shall be the duty of the prosecuting attorney to prosecute in behalf of the Nation all persons charged with criminal offences that may be brought before the court of the Nation, and be required to take the following oath or affirmation: "You do solemly swear that you as prosecuting attorney for and on behalf of the Nation, will, to the best of your skill and ability prosecute all persons charged with criminal offences that may be brought before the court, and that you will not take or receive any remuneration of any person charged with any criminal offence, but will be faithful to the Osage Nation in all prosecutions to the best of your ability, so help you God."

SEC. 34. There shall be a National Secretary, who shall be elected by the council for the term of two years, he shall be clerk of the council and court and shall keep a record of all the proceedings of both the council and court; and perform such other duties that may be provided by law.

ARTICLE XI.

Attorney.

SEC. 35. Before any citizen shall be allowed to appear before the court of this Nation for the purpose of practicing at law he shall obtain a license from the clerk thereof, and pay in advance annually the sum of five dollars to practice before the court, and be required to take an oath that he will to the best of his knowledge and ability support and defend all cases that may be entrusted to his care.

SEC. 36. Any person engaged in the practice of law agree able to the provisions of this act, who shall be convicted before the court of bribing or otherwise influencing any person to keep them from appearing at court, or proving unfaithful to their duties and oaths, shall be subject to a fine of twenty-five dollars, and the revocation of their license. All fines collected under the provision of this act shall be paid into the treasury.

ARTICLE XII.

Lawful Fences.

SEC. 37. A fence nine rails high, with cracks not exceeding four inches wide, for four rails up said fence, and a fence seven good rails high well staked and ridered, shall also be considered a lawful fence, and a board or wire fence four feet high with post eight feet apart, shall also be a lawful fence; and any stock whatever, that may breake into the field of any person or persons having a lawful fence, the owner of such property shall be responsible for the damages done.

ARTICLE XIII.

AN ACT *prohibiting the sale of timber and stone.*

SEC. 38. No person or persons shall be allowed to sell to citizens of the United States any timber, rails, boards, or stones, under the penalty of being liable to a fine in a sum of not less than twenty-five nor exceeding fifty dollars for every such offence, or in default of payment shall be imprisoned for any term not exceeding thirty days at the discretion of the court.

ARTICLE XIV.

Permits to employ or rent to U. S. citizen.

SEC. 39. Any citizen of this Nation who may desire to employ or rent to a citizen of the United States shall be required to obtain a permit for that purpose from the Osage Council, and be approved by the Indian agent and the Indian Office at Washington.

SEC. 40. For all such permits granted the national secretary shall require of the person obtaining it one dollar for every month or fraction of a month for which it is granted. He shall report to the treasurer at the end of each quarter and turn over to him all the receipts that may come into his hands for the quarter then ending.

SEC. 41. After the expiration of the time of the permits, such person shall be deemed an intruder, and it is made the duty of prosecuting attorney to report the same to the Indian agent.

SEC. 42. Any citizen of this Nation who shall hire or employ any citizen of the United States in any other manner than as provided in the first section of this article shall be deemed guilty of a misdemeanor, and, upon conviction, be fined in any sum not less than twenty-five nor exceeding fifty dollars, at the discretion of the c urt; and in default of payment be imprisoned, not less t an fifteen nor exceeding thirty days. No permits shall be granted longer than one year. Persons holding such permits shall be allowed two span of horses or oxen, two cows and calves, and ten hogs, all stock over this number as above specified shall be taxed.

ARTICLE XV.

Drover's Taxes.

SEC. 43. Every person not a citizen of this Nation, driving stock into this Nation for the purpose of grazing or feeding the same shall be liable to a tax at the rate of five cents a head per month.

SEC. 44. It shall not be lawful for any citizen of this Nation to hold within the limits of the Osage Nation, for the purpose of grazing or feeding, any stock belonging to a citizen of the United States, until first procuring a permit from the National Council for that purpose, and paying a tax as provided by law. Any citizen of this Nation violating the provisions of this act shall be liable to a fine of one hundred dollars, and in default of payment be imprisoned not less than thirty nor more than fifty days.

In all cases where a sheriff or other person acting under lawful authority, has reason to believe that efforts are being made to evade the provisions of this Act by collision of some citizen of this Nation, with the owner of stock, such citizen claiming to be the owner, such sheriff or other person shall require the claimant to exhibit his bill of purchase of the stock in question; if deemed necessary to arrive at the facts, he may put such claimant or any other person supposed to be cognizant of the facts in the premises, upon oath, and question him or them as to the bona fide ownership of such stock, and in all such cases, if it appears that there has bee fraud attempted for the purpose of evading the revenue l. ws of this nation, then and in that case there shall be levied double the amount of tax which would otherwise have been made. All money collected under the provisions of this Act shall be paid into the Treasury.

ARTICLE XVI.

Fixing Compensation of Officers.

SEC. 45. From and after the first Monday of November, 1882, the salary and pay of the following officers and persons in the employ of the Osage Nation shall be as follows. to wit:

Principal Chief	Per annum		$300 00
Assistant Principal Chief	"	"	200 00
Supreme Judges, each	"	"	100 00
Members of National Council, each	"	"	100 00
National Clerk	"	"	200 00
High Sheriff	"	"	100 00
Sheriffs, each	"	"	80 00

Executive Councilors shall each receive a compensation for their services which shall be two dollars per day while in actual service.

CHAPTER III.

ARTICLE I.

AN ACT *relating to the judiciary.*

SECTION 1. That the seat of the Osage Government is hereby established at Pawhuska.

SEC. 2. The court established under the Government of this Nation, shall have jurisdiction of all suits rising under the Constitution and laws of the Osage Nation.

SEC. 3. There shall be established a Supreme Court which shall consist of one Chief Justice, and two associate judges. who shall decide all civil cases.

SEC. 4. It shall be the duty of the three judges to choose two persons of good character and knowledge, who shall in conjunction with them, constitute a court for the purpose of hearing and deciding, all criminal cases. The compensation of persons chosen shall be one dollar and fifty cents per day while in actual service.

SEC. 5. No citizen of the Osage Nation who may be employed by the United States Government, as police, shall be chosen to sit as judge in the court of the Osage Nation.

SEC. 6. The commencement of all suits shall be by summons obtained from the clerk of the court, and which summons shall state the nature of the case upon which proceedings are founded, and be served by some lawful officer at least twenty days before the holding of said court, and such summons shall be returnable to the clerk with a certificate of service, and the court shall give judgment as the right of the cause, and the matter in law shall appear under them without regarding any imperfection, defect or want of form in such summons in process.

ARTICLE II.

Duties of Sheriffs.

SEC. 7. There shall be one Sheriff in each District, who shall enter into bonds with security to the amount of three hundred dollars for the faithful execution of duties of his office, and take the following oath. "I. A. B.," having been elected to the office of Sheriff of —— District, do solemnly swear that I will, well and truly execute the duties of said office; according to the best of my ability, without fraud or partiality. It shall be the duty of the Sheriffs to attend the court to serve all summons or other process, which may be placed in their hands, and to take all necessary and proper measures in the execution of the judgements of the court, and also to arrest and cause to be tried all persons who may be charged with criminal offences, and in case of resistance or strong apprehensions of resistance, the Sheriff shall summons such number of citizens as may be necessary to arrest any person or persons against whom criminal charges may be alleged, and to confine the same in jail until convicted or acquitted; should any person charged with criminal violation of law resist any lawful officer, or person authorized to cause arrest, while in the discharge of his or their duty, and such persons should be killed on account of unlawful resistance, such officer or other person shall not be held guilty of murder.

ARTICLE III.

Relating to District.

The following divisions of the Osage Nation into five districts shall continue until altered by law, to wit:

PAWNEENOPAHSHE DISTRICT.

SEC. 8. Commencing at the Pawnee crossing on the Arkansas River, thence along the old Pawnee road, to the Elm Spring, thence along the Salt Creek road to the top of the dividing ridge between Hominy and Clear Creeks, thence in a direct line to where the Kaw road crosses the flint hills, thence along said flint hills to the State line, thence west along said line to the Kaw boundary, thence along said boundary to the Arkansas River, thence along said river to the place of beginning.

BLACK DOG DISTRICT

SEC. 9. Commencing at the Elm Spring, thence south in a direct line to Prominent mound, thence in a direct line to where the Cherokee line crosses Delaware creek, thence south along said line to the Arkansas river, thence up said river to the Pawnee crossing, thence bounded by the first district.

CLAMMORE DISTRICT.

SEC. 10. Commencing at the top of the dividing ridge, between Hominy and Clear creeks, thence east along said division to where the Cherokee line crosses Bird creek, thence south along said line to Delaware creek, to be bounded on the south by the Second, and on the west by the First districts.

PAWHUSKA DISTRICT.

SEC. 11. Commencing where the Cherokee line crosses Bird creek, thence north along said line to Sand creek, thence west in a direct line to Gus Strikeaxe's place, between Mission and Rock creeks, thence in a direct line to where the Elgin road crosses Rock creek, thence in a direct line to the flint hills at the head of Bird creek, to be bounded on the west by the First, and on the south by the Third districts.

STRIKEAX DISTRICT.

SEC. 12. Commencing where the Cherokee line crosses Sand creek, thence along said line north to the State line, thence along said line to the Flint hills, thence along said hills to the head of Bird creek, to be bounded on the south by the Fourth district.

Resolved by the National Council:

SEC. 13. That we accept the sum of one hundred (100) dollars per year from the Indian agent in charge, in full for all salaries due us for services as members of the Osage Council, and that we ask the judges of the Osage Nation to accept one hundred (100) dollars per annum in full for their services as judges of the Osage Nation, to be paid as aforesaid, also, that all other officers whose salaries are prescribed at a stated amount per annum, be asked to receive thereby as above; all of the above salaries to be paid from our tribal funds in the hands of the United States Government.

Provided, That all the aforesaid officers shall receipt for the same in full for all moneys due them as officers of this nation, for the time for which they are paid.

Approved March 4th, 1882.

(SIGNED,) JOSEPH PAW-NE-NO-PAN-SHE,
Principal Chief.

E. M. MATHEWS, *Secretary.*

CONSTITUTION AND LAWS

OF THE

SAC AND FOX NATION

INDIAN TERRITORY.

The Constitution of the Sac and Fox Nation, Prepared by the Authorized Committee, and Adopted by the National Council.

ST. LOUIS AND NEW YORK.
PRESS OF THE AUGUST GAST BANK NOTE & LITHO. CO.
1888.

CONSTITUTION.

THE CONSTITUTION OF THE SAC AND FOX NATION, PREPARED BY THE AUTHORIZED COMMITTEE AND ADOPTED BY THE NATIONAL COUNCIL:

The Sac and Fox tribes of Indians having united and become one body politic as long ago as the year 1804, under the style and title of the Sac and Fox tribe of Indians of the Mississippi, therefore—

We, the people of the Sac and Fox tribe of Indians of the Mississippi, in National Council assembled, in order to extend the benefits of our National Government, as provided for in section 9, of our treaty with the United States, proclaimed October 14, 1868, to establish justice, insure tranquility, promote the common welfare and secure to ourselves and our posterity the blessings of freedom —-acknowledging the humility and gratitude the goodness of the Sovereign Ruler of the universe in permitting us so to do, and imploring His aid and guidance in its accomplishment—do ordain and establish this Constitution for the Goverment of the Sac and Fox tribe of Indians of the Mississippi, to be called and known as the SAC AND FOX NATION:

ARTICLE I.

SECTION 1. The lands of the Sac and Fox Nation are those provided by the treaty of October 14, 1868, between the United States and the Sac and Fox tribe of Indians of the Mississippi, comprising 479,667 acres lying in the Indian Territory next west of the Creek Nation, the Cimarron river forming the north and the North Fork Canadian river the south lines thereof.

SEC. 2. The lands of the Sac and Fox Nation shall remain common property, but the improvements made thereon and in possession of the citizens of the Nation are the exclusive and indefeasible property of the citizens respectively who made or may rightfully be in possession of them. *Provided:* That the citizens of this Nation possessing exclusive and indefeasible right to their improvements, as expressed in this article, shall possess no right or power to dispose of their improvements whatever, to the United States, individual States, or to individual citizens thereof; and that whenever any citizen shall remove without the limits of this Nation with his effects and become a citizen of any other government, all his rights and privileges as a citizen of this Nation shall cease. *Provided, nevertheless,* That the National Council shall have power to readmit by law to all the rights of citizenship any such persons who may at any time desire to return to the Nation, on memorializing the National Council for such readmission. *Provided, further*, That nothing in this section shall be construed to include to include property right. Moreover the National Council shall have power to adopt such laws and regulations as it may deem expedient and proper to prevent citizens from monopolizing improvements with the view of speculation.

ARTICLE II.

SECTION 1. The power of this government shall be divided into three distinct departments, the Legislative, the Executive, and the Judicial.

SEC. 2. No person belonging to one of these departments shall exercise any of the powers properly belonging to either of the others, except in the cases hereinafter expressly directed or permitted.

ARTICLE III.

SECTION 1. The Legislative power shall be vested in a National Council, and the style of their acts shall be: Be it enacted by the National Council.

SEC. 2. The National Council shall consist of five members from each band, to-wit: The treaty chiefs and two councillors each, of their own choosing, and two additional members from each band, to be elected or selected by each band respectively, the councillors chosen and the last mentioned members to be elected as may be provided by law; each shall serve a term of two years.

SEC. 3. The National Council shall, after the present year, be held annually, to convene on the first Monday in October, at such place as may be designated by the National Council, or, in case of emergency, by the principal chief.

SEC. 4. The first election for all officers of the government—Principal and Assistant Principal Chiefs, Executive Council, members of the National Council, Judges and Sheriffs—shall be held at Sac and Fox Agency before the rising of this Council, and the term of service of all officers elected shall be extended to embrace the time intervening from their election to the first Monday in October, 1886.

SEC. 5. No person shall be eligible to a seat in the National Council but Sac and Fox male citizens who shall have attained the age of twenty-five years.

SEC. 6. The members of the National Council shall in all cases, except those of felony or breach of the peace, be privileged from arrest during their attendance at the National Council, in going to or returning therefrom.

SEC. 7. All officers of this Nation shall be elected by the National Council every two years, except as hereinbefore provided, as to the members of the National Council, immediately after the organization of each biennial Council.

SEC. 8 In elections by the people the electors shall vote *viva voce*. All male citizens who shall have attained the age of eighteen years shall be equally entitled to vote at all public elections.

SEC. 9. The National Council shall judge of the qualifications and returns of its own members, determine the rules of its proceedings, punish a member for disorderly behavior, and with the concurrence of two-thirds, expel a member.

SEC. 10. The National Council, when assembled, shall choose its own officers; a majority shall constitute a quorum to do business, but a smaller number may adjourn from day to day, and compel the attendance of absent members in such manner and under such penalty as the Council may prescribe.

SEC. 11. The National Council is empowered to fix by law the salaries of all officers of the Nation and members of the National Council, except that of the treaty chiefs, who shall receive no other salary than that provided by the treaty of October 14, 1868. *Provided*, That the same are increased or diminished by law, but no other alteration shall take effect during the period of service of the members of the National Council by whom such alteration may have been made.

SEC. 12. The National Council shall regulate by law by whom and in what manner writs of election shall be issued to fill vacancies which may happen in the Council thereof.

SEC. 13. Each member of the National Council, before he takes his seat, shall take the following oath or affirmation:

I, A. B., do solemnly swear (or affirm, as the case may be) that I have not obtained my election by bribery, threat, or any undue and unlawful means, used by myself, or others by my desire or approbation for that purpose: that I consider myself constitutionally qualified as a member of the National Council, and that on all questions and measures which may come before me I will so give my vote and conduct myself as, in my judgment, shall appear most conducive to the interest and prosperity of this Nation: and that I will bear true faith and allegiance to the same, and to the utmost of my ability and power observe, conform to, support and defend the constitution thereof.

SEC. 14. No person who may be convicted of felony shall be eligible to any office of appointment or honor, profit or trust within this Nation.

SEC. 15. The National Council shall have power to make all laws and regulations which they shall deem necessary and proper for the good of the Nation, which shall not be contrary to this constitution.

SEC. 16. It shall be the duty of the National Council to pass such laws as may be necessary and proper to decide differences by arbitration, to be appointed by the parties who may choose that summary mode of adjustment.

SEC. 17. No power of suspending the laws of this Nation shall be exercised, unless by the National Council or its authority.

SEC. 18. No retroactive law nor any law impairing the obligation of contracts, shall be passed.

SEC. 19. The National Council shall have power to make laws for levying and collecting taxes for the purpose of raising a revenue.

SEC. 20. All acknowledged treaties shall be the supreme law of the land, and the National Council shall have the sole power of deciding on the constructions of treaty stipulations.

SEC. 21. The Council shall have the sole power of impeaching. All impeachments shall be tried by the National Council, when sitting for that purpose; the members shall be upon oath or affirmation; and no person shall be convicted without the concurrence of two-thirds of the members present.

SEC. 22. The Principal Chief, Assistant Principal Chief, and all civil officers shall be liable to impeachment for misdemeanor in office; but judgment in such cases shall not extend further than removal from office and disqualification to hold any office of honor, trust or profit under the government of this Nation. The party, whether convicted or acquitted, shall be liable to indictment, trial, judgment and punishment according to law.

ARTICLE IV.

SECTION 1. The supreme executive power of this Nation shall be vested in a Principal Chief, who shall be styled "THE PRINCIPAL CHIEF OF THE SAC AND FOX NATION." The Principal Chief, shall hold his office for the term of two years, and shall be elected by the National Council from the treaty chiefs on the organization of each biennial Council.

SEC. 2. No person except a native born citizen shall be eligible to the office of Principal Chief; neither shall any person be eligible to that office who shall not have attained the age of thirty-five years.

SEC. 3. There shall be chosen at the same time by the National Council, in the same manner, for two years, an Assistant Principal Chief, who shall have attained the age of thirty-five years.

SEC. 4. In case of the removal of the Principal Chief from office, or of his death or resignation, or inability to discharge the powers and duties of the said office, the same shall devolve upon the Assistant Principal Chief, who shall be one of the treaty chiefs.

SEC. 5. The National Council may by law provide for the case of removal, death, resignation, or disability of both the Principal and Assistant Principal Chiefs, declaring what officer shall then act as Principal Chief, until the disability be removed, or a Principal Chief shall be elected.

SEC. 6. The Principal Chief, and Assistant Principal Chief shall receive for their services no other compensation than that provided in the treaty of 1868, and they shall not receive within that period any other emolument from the Sac and Fox Nation or any other government.

SEC. 7. Before the Principal Chief enters upon the execution of his office he shall take the following oath or affirmation: "I do solemnly swear (or affirm) that I will faithfully execute the duties of Principal Chief of the Sac and Fox Nation, and will, to the best of my ability, preserve, protect and defend the Constitution of the Sac and Fox Nation."

SEC. 8. He may, on extraordinary occasions, convene the National Council at the seat of the government.

SEC. 9. He shall, from time to time, give to the Council information of the state of the government, and recommend to their consideration such measures as he may deem expedient.

SEC. 10. He shall take care that the laws be faithfully executed.

SEC. 11 It shall be his duty to visit the different bands at least once in two years, to inform himself of the condition of the country.

SEC. 12. The Assistant Principal Chief shall, by virtue of his office, aid and advise the Principal Chief in the administration of the government at all times during his continuance in office.

SEC. 13. Vacancies that may occur in offices, the appointment of which is vested in the National Council, shall be filled by the Principal Chief during the recess of the National Council, by granting commission, which shall expire at the end of the next session thereof.

SEC. 14. Every bill which shall pass the National Council, shall, before it becomes a law, be presented to the Principal Chief; if he approves he shall sign it, but if not he shall return it with his objections to the Council, who shall enter them at large on their journal, and proceed to reconsider it. If, after such reconsideration, two-thirds of the Council shall agree to pass the bill, it becomes a law. If any bill shall not be returned by the Principal Chief within five days (Sunday excepted) after the same has been presented to him, it shall become a law in like manner as if he had signed it, unless the National Council, by their adjournment prevent its return, in which case it shall be a law unless sent back within three days after their next meeting.

SEC. 15. Members of the National Council and all officers, executive and judicial, shall be bound by oath to support the Constitution of their Nation, and to perform the duties of their respective offices with fidelity.

SEC. 16. The Principal Chief shall, during the session of the National Council, attend at the seat of government.

SEC. 17. There shall be an Executive Council composed of the treaty chiefs and their Councillors, who, or a majority of whom, may from time to time hold and keep a Council for ordering and directing the affairs of the Nation according to law.

SEC. 18. The Treasurer of the Sac and Fox Nation shall be chosen by the National Council for a term of two years.

SEC. 19. The Treasurer may be a member of the National Council and Treasurer at the same time, but he shall not receive the pay of but one of said offices.

SEC. 20. The Treasurer shall, before entering upon the duties of his office, give bond to the Nation with sureties to the satisfaction of the National Council for the faithful discharge of his trust.

SEC. 21. No money shall be drawn from the treasury but by warrant from the Principal Chief, and in consequence of appropriations made by law.

SEC. 22. It shall be the duty of the Treasurer to receive all public moneys, and to make a regular statement and account of the receipts and expenditures of all puplic moneys at the annual session of the National Council.

SEC. 23. The fiscal year of the Sac and Fox Nation shall begin on the first day of October, and close on the 30th day of September of each year; and all books and accounts of the Treasurer shall be kept, and duties of the office performed, with regard to the beginning and ending of the fiscal year. The National Treasurer's salary may be fixed by law.

ARTICLE V.

SECTION 1. The judicial powers shall be vested in a Supreme Court, and such circuit and inferior courts as the National Council may from time to time ordain and establish.

Sec. 2. The Judges of the Supreme and Circuit Courts shall hold their commissions for the term of two years, but any of them may be removed from office on the address of two-thirds of the National Council to the Principal Chief for that purpose.

Sec. 3. The salary of the Judges of the Supreme and Circuit Courts may be fixed by law, which shall not be diminished during their continuance in office, but they shall receive no fees or perquisites of office, nor hold any other office of profit or trust under the government of this Nation or any other power.

Sec. 4. No person shall be appointed a Judge of any of the courts until he shall have attained the age of thirty years.

Sec. 5. The Judges of the Supreme and inferior Courts shall be elected by the National Council.

Sec. 6. The Judges of the Supreme and Circuit Courts shall have complete criminal jurisdiction in such cases and in such manner as may be pointed out by law.

Sec. 7. No judge shall sit on trial of any cause when the parties are connected with him by affinity or consanguinity, except by consent of the parties. In case all the court (Supreme) shall be interested in the issue of any court, or related to all or either of the parties, the National Council may provide by law for the selection of a suitable number of persons of good character and knowledge for the determination thereof, and who shall be specially commissioned for the adjudication of such case by the Principal Chief.

Sec. 8. All writs and other process shall run "in the name of the Sac and Fox Nation," and bear attest and be signed by the respective clerks.

Sec. 9. Indictments shall conclude "against the peace and dignity of the Sac and Fox Nation."

Sec. 10. The place and meetings of the different courts shall be determined by the National Council.

Sec. 11. In all criminal prosecutions the accused shall have the right of being heard; of demanding the nature of the accusation; of meeting the witnesses face to face; of having compulsory process for obtaining witnesses in his or their behalf, and in prosecutions by indictments or information a speedy public trial; nor shall the accused be compelled to give evidence against himself.

Sec. 12. All persons shall be bailable by sufficient securities, unless for capital offenses when the proof is evident or presumption great.

ARTICLE VI.

SECTION 1. No person who denies the being of a God, or a future state of reward or punishment shall hold any office in the civil department of this Nation.

SEC. 2. When the Executive Council, or a majority of them, shall determine the expediency of appointing delegates, or other public agents, for the purpose of transacting business with the government of the United States, and other parties, the Principal Chief shall recommend, and, by the advice and consent of the Executive Council, or a majority of them, appoint and commission such delegates or public agents accordingly, on all matters of interest touching the rights or interest of the citizens of this Nation. The compensation of such delegates or agents shall be determined by the Council.

SEC. 3. All persons shall be allowed the right of counsel.

SEC. 4. All commissions shall be in the name and by the authority of the Sac and Fox Nation, and signed by the Principal Chief. The Principal Chief shall make use of his private seal until a National one shall be provided.

SEC. 5. A Sheriff shall be elected by the National Council, who shall hold his office two years, unless sooner removed. Should a vacancy occur subsequent to election, it shall be filled by the Principal Chief, as in other cases, and the person so appointed shall continue in office until the next regular election. The Sheriff shall have the power to appoint as many as one under Sheriff from each band.

SEC. 6. The appointment of all officers not otherwise directed by this Constitution shall be voted for in National Council.

SEC. 7. The National Council may propose such amendments to this Constitution as two-thirds of the Council may deem expedient, and the Principal Chief shall issue a proclamation directing all officers of the several bands to promulgate the same as extensively as possible within their respective bands at least six months previous to the next general election, and if at the first session of the Council after such general election, two-thirds of the Council shall by ayes and noes ratify such proposed amendments, they shall be valid to all extent and purposes, as part of this Constitution. *Provided*, That such proposed amendments shall be read on three several days in Council, as well as when the same are proposed as when they are ratified.

Done in Convention at Sac and Fox Agency, Sac and Fox Nation, this 26th day of MARCH, A. D. 1885.

UCQUAW HO KO, his X mark,	MAHKO SAH TOE, his X mark,
NUL LAH KE, his X mark,	HENRY CLAY JONES,
ALEX CONNOLLY,	KEOKUK, his X mark,
NOM MOL WAH, his X mark,	WILLIAM HARRIS,
ANTOINE GOKEY,	MILTON CARTER,
CHARLES KEOKUK,	MY AW CHE, his X mark,
WAW PE KO HAL, his X mark,	CUP PAW HE, his X mark,
KE OM MO WHAT, his X mark,	KAH CHE PIM MO SAH, hisXmark
MAH KO KAW, his X mark,	WAW PAW KO HUCK, hisXmark
SHOW-QUE-QUOT, his X mark,	TUS-SE-HAW, his X mark,
WAW-KAL-LE, his X mark,	MAW MAL LE HAW, his X mark,

KISH KE TEN O KAH.

At a full Council of the Chiefs and head men of the Sac and Fox tribe of Indians of the Mississippi, in the Indian Territory, held in their Council House at Sac and Fox Agency, I. T., on this the 14th day of March, A. D. 1885, the following proceedings were had, to-wit:

After a full and fair discussion as to the advisabillity of the Sac and Fox tribe of Indians of the Mississippi, in the Indian Territory, organizing a civil form of government for their future government, it was decided that in such a course there was wisdom and an imperative demand therefor.

Therefore it was resolved by said Council that a committee consisting of seven members of their tribe be appointed by said Council to draft a suitable constitution and laws looking to that end, to be submitted to a regular Council to be held on the 26th day of March, A. D. 1885. The Council appointed as said committee, Wm. Harris, Mah-ko-se-toe Nish-koh-kat, Mash-ko-kah, Show-que quat, Nom-wol-wah and Robert Thrift.

Council adjourned to meet March 26, 1885, at Council room of Sac and Fox Agency.

CHAS. KEOKUK.

March 14, 1885. *Secretary.*

SAC AND FOX AGENCY, I. T. March 26, 1885.

Council met pursuant to adjournment. Committee submitted report as per the appended Constitution, which was fully discussed and adopted. Said committee submitted also a code of laws, which was received and laid over until April 6, 1885, for action by the Council.

MEMBERS PRESENT:

1. UC QUAW HO KO, *Head Chief.*

KEOKUK,	Chief,	KE OM LO WHAT,	Headman.
CHE KO SUK,	"	MASH KO KAW,	"
CUP PAW HE,	"	SHOW QUE QUAT,	"
WAH KO MO,	"	KIS KE TEN O KAH,	"
MAH KO SE TOE,	Headman,	ANTOINE GOKEY,	"
WAH PE KO HOL,	"	BLACK NECK,	"
NUL LAH KE,	"	KAH CAE PIM MO SAH,	"
MAW MAL LE HAW,	"	WAW PAW KO HUCK,	"
NOM MOL WAH,	"	MY AW CHE,	"
WAW KAL LE,	"	TUS SE HAW,	"
MILTON CARTER,	"	NISH KO KAT,	"

Adjourned to meet at Council room, April 6, 1885, Sac and Fox Agency, I. T.

CHAS. KEOKUK,
Secretary.

March 26, 1885.

SAC AND FOX AGENCY, I. T., April 6, 1885.

Council met pursuant to adjournment. All the members being present. The laws for the government of the Sac and Fox tribe as reported by committee, was then discussed and adopted by a three-fifths vote, said adoption being by a vote upon each act, by section seventeen, and then as a whole, until all acts hereto appended were adopted.

The following officers were unanimously elected, to-wit:

UC QUAW HO KO, *Principal Chief,* KEOKUK, *Ass't Prin. Chief.*
WM. HARRIS, *Treasurer.* ROBT. THRIFT, *Pros. Att'y.*
ALEX. CONNOLLY, *Sheriff,* H. C. JONES, *Dis't Judge.*
ADDITIONAL COUNCILLORS:—WAH PE KO HAL, MAW MAL LE HAW, MILTON CARTER, ANTOINE GOKEY, MASH KO KAW, WAW PAW KO-HUCK, KISH KE TEN O KAH, TUS SE HAW.

Resolutions passed asking U. S. Indian Agent, I. A. Taylor, to forward copy of Constitution and laws to the Hon. Commissioner of Indian Affairs for approval. Council adjourned.

CHAS. KEOKUK,
Treasurer.

April 6, 1885.

LAWS OF THE
SAC AND FOX NATION.

CHAPTER 2—ARTICLE 1.

An Act for the Punishment of Criminal Offences.

SEC. 1. That in all cases of wilful murder, the offender upon trial and conviction by the authorized Court of this Nation, shall suffer death by hanging or shooting, and when the sentence of death shall have been passed, the court shall grant a respite of five days, before such criminal shall be executed. *Provided*, That if any such offender plead guilty before the court trying the same, said offender shall be sentenced to solitary confinement at hard labor in the prison that may at that time be provided by this Nation for a term less than fifty years.

SEC. 2. That any person who shall, with malice aforethought, assault another with intent to kill, shall upon conviction thereof be fined in a sum for the benefit of the party injured, not less than five nor more than fifty dollars, at the discretion of the court, and receive not less than twenty-five nor more than fifty lashes on the bare back. But if any person shall kill in self-defence or by accident, without any previous intent to do the same, he shall not be held accountable for such act, and be exempt from any fine or punishment whatever.

SEC. 3. Any person who is or may be convicted of threating to kill another shall be adjudged to pay a fine of not more than fifty dollars, and to receive fifty lashes on his bare back.

SEC 4. That upon trial and conviction of any person charged with the offense of having committed or an attempt to commit a rape on any female, he shall be punished with not less than twenty-five nor more than fifty lashes on the bare back.

ARTICLE II.

An act for the punishment of thefts and other crimes.

SEC. 1. That any person who shall be convicted of stealing a horse, mule, jack or jennet, shall be punished by not less than thirty nor more than fifty lashes on the bare back, and be compelled to make payment to the amount of damages or injuries sustained, if such stolen property be not restored, for the benefit of the person so injured; and for all other property which shall be in proportion to the magnitude of the offense, at the discretion of the court, and judgment against the offender for damages to the party injured.

SEC. 2. That if any person shall wilfully and maliciously burn the house or other property of another or otherwise kill any animal or destroy the property of any person for the purpose of injury or gratifying a spirit of revenge, or otherwise, shall be punished in like manner as provided in the section above, and be compelled to make ample remuneration by such compensation as the court may determine.

SEC. 3. Any person who shall wilfully or knowingly mark or brand any animal, the property of another, with a mark or brand not that of the owner without the consent of said owner, or authority of law, or shall knowingly alter or deface the mark or brand of any animal not his own, without the consent of such owner, shall upon conviction thereof, be punished by a fine of not less than fifteen or more than fifty dollars.

SEC. 4. Any person convicted of breaking into any house, corncrib, smokehouse or stable, with intent to steal anything therefrom, or any person stealing any property therefrom at any time, shall be punished by fine not less than ten dollars or more than fifty dollars or by imprisonment in the National prison not more than sixty days or by both such fine and imprisonment in the discretion of the court.

SEC. 5. Any person who shall, at any time or in any place play at any game for gain with cards, dice, or any device which may be used or adapted to playing any game of chance or hazard, or shall bet on the hands or sides of those who do play, within one mile of the Sac and Fox Agency, or Sac and Fox M. L. School, or any public gathering, shall be deemed guilty of a misdemeanor, and shall be fined in a sum not less than five dollars, nor exceeding twenty-five dollars.

SEC. 6. That any person convicted of introducing intoxicating liquors of any kind on or into the Sac and Fox reservation shall be fined fifty dollars, and should any person be injured physically thereby, the fine shall be an additional seventy dollars, or imprisonment for a term not more than one year or both such fine and imprisonment in the discretion of the court. *Provided*, That any person giving information to the authorities of the place where any intoxicating liquors may be found on the reservation unlawfully in possession of any person, the person so informing shall be paid ten dollars for such information. *Provided, further*, That such information leads to the arrest and conviction of the person owning or possessing said liquors. And, *Provided, further*, That any citizen of the United States so introducing said intoxicating liquors on the Sac and Fox reservation, shall be arrested and turned over to the United States authorities for trial.

SEC. 7. Any person convicted of stealing garden produce shall be fined two dollars, and also pay to the injured party the full value of the produce so stolen; the value thereof to be ascertained by the Sheriff who reports the same to the court before which the accused may be tried.

SEC. 8. Any person being in a state of intoxication on the Sac and Fox reservation shall, upon conviction thereof, before the court of this Nation, be fined for each offense the sum of not less than two dollars nor more than twenty-five dollars, as the court may direct, or may be imprisoned not less than ten days or more than sixty days, or by both such fine and imprisonment in the discretion of the court.

SEC. 9. All fines provided for in these laws shall be paid over to the Treasurer, by the Secretary of the Nation, for the use of the Nation.

ARTICLE III.

Disturbing Public Assemblies.

SEC. 9. Every person who shall wilfully annoy, by word or deed or in any manner disturbs any school, religious or social public meeting, lawfully assembled, upon conviction thereof shall be fined not less than five dollars nor more than fifty dollars. And that the members of every religious and social public meeting, when lawfully assembled, be authorized to adopt such measures for the peace and harmony of their meeting, by the suppression of the sale and indulgence in the use of intoxicating drinks, and for the preservation of peace, as may seem to them most proper and best suited to that purpose, and said assembly, or the individual members thereof, shall not be responsible for any damages suffered by persons, in the exercise of the right herein granted.

Sec. 9. That any person who shall employ another, or aid or abet in the perpetration of any criminal offense, upon conviction thereof, such person or persons shall suffer such punishment as may be inflicted upon the principal offender and be likewise subject to the same judgment for damages.

ARTICLE IV.

Miscellaneous Official Bonds.

Sec. 1. That hereafter, it shall be unlawful for this council to approve of any person, as surety upon any official bond, unless such surety furnish the Secretary of the Nation with a list of the personal property he owns in his own name, and should such surety at any time hereafter, dispose of his property, for the purpose, or to the effect of defrauding the Nation out of any portion of his liability upon such bond, he shall upon conviction be guilty of a misdemeanor, and punished by fine not exceeding $100 or imprisonment not exceeding six months, or both, as the court may direct.

Sec. 2. That should any National officer become a defaulter to the Nation, suit may be brought in the Supreme Court against said Officer and his sureties, upon his bond, and the same may be declared forfeited and judgment entered in said court for the amount found to be due the Nation by said officer, and execution shall issue and shall in all respects be treated as executions are in other cases.

Sec. 3. That if any principal or surety upon any official bond at any time disposes of his property in anticipation of a defalcation of the officer whose bond he signed, the Sheriff may attach such property and hold the same until the amount of defalcation be ascertained by the court, and then proceed according to law with said property.

ESTRAYS.

Sec. 1. That any person taking up stray horses, hogs, cattle or other stock, shall notify the Secretary within five days, giving to that officer a true and correct description of the same, and also state where such stock may be seen and the name of the person taking up the same.

Sec. 2. It shall be the duty of the National Secretary immediately upon receiving such information to post the same on the door of Council-house by writing a full and correct description thereof, together with the name and residence of the person taking up said stock, and asking the owner or owners thereof to proceed to prove their property, pay all charges, and take the same away, as hereinafter provided.

Sec. 3. Any person claiming to be the owner of such stray stock, may notify the person so taking up said strays, that he or they will appear on a certain day, not less than two days thereafter, unless a shorter time be agreed upon, before one of the Judges of the National Court and prove his ownership to the said stock.

SEC. 4. If any such person proves to be the owner of such stock, the said Judge shall order and decree that such owner shall, upon payment of two dollars for each month or fractional part thereof, receive such stock that the person taking up such stray has had said stock, counting from the day said Secretary was notified that said stock was taken up; one-half of said charges to be paid to the person taking up said stray, and the other half is to be paid to the National Secretary, and by him paid into the National Treasury.

SEC. 5. Should any strays so taken up remain in the possession of the person so taking up the same for the space of one year, without having been proven up as aforesaid, then, said person taking up such stray, shall notify the National Secretary of the same, who shall advertise the same for the term of thirty days, and if the same is not claimed by any one, or proven up as aforsaid, the same shall be sold by the Sheriff, who shall summon three men, members of this nation, to appraise said stock, and if the person so taking up said stock shall pay to the National Secretary, for the use of the National Treasury, one-half of said appraised value, he shall be held and deemed to be the legal owner thereof thereafter.

SEC. 6. Any person who shall dispose of or wilfully take any stray property not his own, or shall wilfully kill or maim any such property, either before or after such property is posted, shall be deemed guilty of the same offense as if the act was committed upon the property of a citizen, and shall, upon conviction, be punished accordingly.

SEC. 7. All laws or parts of laws inconsistent herewith are hereby repealed.

FENCES.

SEC. 1. All eight-rail worm fences, staked and ridered with single rider, and all wire fences of four wires not to exceed ten inches apart, and posts not to exceed fifteen feet apart, shall be deemed and held to be a lawful fence. Any stock breaking into or through such fence and doing any damage to growing crops, trees or shrubs, may be held by the person so trespassed upon, until all damages said stock may have done, be paid by the owner of said stock, to the party so injured. The amount of such damage shall be appraised by the Sheriff, who shall report the amount of such damages to the Judge of the Supreme Court, and said Judge shall enter the amount upon the records of said court, and the same shall be a judgment against the owner of said stock. *Provided*, That the parties in interest may make settlement amicably for any amount, which settlement so made shall be a full satisfaction of any such judgment.

SEC. 2. Any person or persons who may be convicted of cutting or in any way injuring any such fence, shall be fined the sum of twenty dollars for each offense.

STOCK IN TRANSIT.

SEC. 2. That, hereafter, all persons not citizens of this Nation who may drive any horses, cattle, mules or other stock through the Sac and Fox reservation, shall pay to the Sheriff of said Nation the sum of two cents per head for each day or fraction thereof said stock may remain on said reservation; said tax to be paid by the Sheriff to the Secretary for the benefit of the National Treasury.

COLLECTION OF DEBTS.

SEC. 3. That any citizen of Sac and Fox blood, of the Sac and Fox Nation in the Indian Territory, and no others, may enforce the collection of any debt arising from contract, damage or forfeiture, or for the recovery of specific personal property, by prosecuting the same before the Supreme Court by a civil action at law.

SEC. 4. All such actions shall be commenced by filing with the clerk of said court a written statement of the cause of action, and a summons shall issue thereon as provided in section six (6) of Article one (1) of Chapter three (3) of Sac and Fox laws.

SEC. 5. After the court hears all the evidence offered by both parties, it shall proceed to enter judgment in favor of the prevailing party and shall enforce the same by issuing an execution directed to the Sheriff of said Nation, who shall serve the same by levying upon the property of the judgment debtor, and after giving ten days' public notice, posted at the Council House in a public place of the time of selling said property at public auction to the highest bidder for cash, and pay the same over to the clerk of said court, who shall pay the same over to the party entitled to receive it.

SEC. 6. No judgment shall be entered by any of the courts of this Nation unless the action thereon shall have been commenced within two years from the date at which the cause of action accrued. *Provided*, No judgment shall be entered upon any debt that was in existence prior to the taking effect of this law, and, *Provided, further*, That all assignments of claims or notes by white men to Indians shall be void and of no effect, and that no judgment shall be entered thereon under this law.

SEC. 7. That the provisions of this act apply to the collection of all taxes and fines under the laws of this Nation as far as applicable.

SALARIES OF OFFICERS.

SEC. 8. That, hereafter, the salaries of the officers of the Sac and Fox Nation, shall, until otherwise provided, be that contained in this act. The salary of the Chief Justice shall be Four hundred dollars per year and no more; and that of the Associate Judges shall be four dollars per day for each day actually employed in attending upon the duties of said office, and no more. The salary of the Treasurer shall be four hundred dollars and no more. The salary of the Secretary shall be four hundred dollars per year and no more. The Prosecuting Attorney's salary shall be three hundred dollars a year and no more. The salary of the Sheriff shall be three hundred dollars per year and no more, *Provided*, That the Deputy Sheriffs shall receive the sum of two (2) dollars per day for each day actually employed on official duty and no more.

SEC. 9. That the salaries of the Eight Executive Councilmen shall be the sum of four dollars each per day or fraction thereof while in session, and no more. And the salaries of the eight elected Councilmen shall be the sum of three dollars per day, or fraction thereof, for the time actually in session and no more.

SEC. 10. All other acts, or parts of acts in conflict with this act, be, and the same are hereby repealed.

DESCENT AND DISTRIBUTION.

SEC. 11. Any person dying in this Nation possessed of property ot any kind, without making a will and leaving a wife or husband, or a child or children without a husband or wife, the said property shall be inherited in the following manner, and no other: The husband or wife and child or children in the order herein named, or, such person dying not having a husband or wife or any children, said property shall descend to the next of kin living.

SEC. 12. All such descents shall be in equal quantities of the same time of decent.

GUARDIANS.

SEC. 13. The oldest blood relation living who can give a good bond for the faithful performance of the trust to the Judges of the Supreme Court, shall be, by either of said Judges appointed the guardian of the person and property of any orphan minor child.

SEC. 14. And if none of the blood relations of any such minor take out letters of guardianship within thirty days, the Principal Chief may designate some suitable person in writing to a Judge of said court who may be appointed such guardian and upon filing with said Judge a good and sufficient bond, as above provided, such guardian shall enter upon the duties of his said office, *Provided*, That each and every guardian be required to make at least one settlement each year, with said court, and as many others as said court may demand, and, *Provided*, *further*, said guardian may be removed at any time for cause, and a proper person appointed as aforesaid to complete the trust.

ARTICLE V.

Employment of Non-Citizens.

SEC. 15. Any Citizen of this Nation who may desire to employ, for one month, or more, or rent to a citizen of the United States, shall be required to obtain a permit for that purpose from the Sac and Fox Executive Council, and be approved by the Indian Agent, and the Indian Office at Washington.

SEC. 16. Any citizen of this Nation who may desire to employ or rent to a non-citizen Indian, shall be required to obtain a permit for that purpose from the Sac and Fox Executive Council, and be approved by the Indian Agent.

SEC. 17. For all such permits granted, the National Secretary shall require of the person obtaining it one dollar for every month or fraction more than a month for which it is granted. He shall report to the Treasurer at the end of each quarter, and turn over to him all of the receipts that may come into his hands for the quarter then ending.

SEC. 18. After the expiration of the time of the permits, such persons shall be deemed an intruder, and it is made the duty of the Prosecuting Attorney to report the same to the Indian Agent.

Sec. 19. Any citizen of this Nation who shall hire or employ any citizen of the United States, or non-citizen Indian, in any other manner than as provided in the first and second sections of this article, shall be deemed guilty of a misdemeanor, and, upon conviction, be fined in any sum not less than twenty-five nor exceeding fifty dollars, at the discretion of the court.

Sec. 20. That any person fined at any time, upon the Sac and Fox reservation, not a citizen of the Nation, or a United States officer or employe, and not having a permit from the Executive Council, and paid for the same according to law, shall be ejected from the reservation as the law directs in other cases.

ARTICLE VI.

Persons who may be Summoned by an Officer.

Sec. 21. No permits shall be granted longer than one year. Persons holding such permits shall be allowed in the discretion of the Executive Council, two span of horses or oxen, two cows and calves but no more or other stock.

Sec. 22. All laws or parts of laws inconsistent with these amendments and this act be and the same are hereby repealed.

Sec. 23. Any person or persons who may be summoned to appear before the court to give in testimony, and shall refuse or fail to attend, unless on account of sickness or other lawful excuse, such persons shall be fined in a sum not less than twenty-five nor more than fifty dollars at the discretion of the court; and any person who may be summoned by an officer to aid in the arrest of any criminal, and shall refuse, unless it shall be on account of sickness, or other lawful excuse, shall be fined twenty-five dollars.

ARTICLE VII.

Resisting Officers.

Sec. 24. Any person who shall resist, abuse, or injure any officer of this Nation, who is in the legal discharge of his duties, shall upon conviction receive for each offense not less than twenty-five nor more than fifty lashes upon the bare back, at the discretion of the court.

ARTICLE VIII.

Destroying Pecan Trees.

Sec. 25. Any person who shall cut down or destroy any pecan tree, for the purpose of obtaining the fruit thereof, shall be fined in the sum of twenty-five dollars.

ARTICE IX.

To legalize intermarriage with white men.

Sec. 26. Any white man or citizen of the United States, who may hereafter come into the Sac and Fox Nation to marry a Sac or Fox woman, shall first be required to make known his intentions to the National Council by applying for a license, and such license may, under the authority of the National Council, be issued by the Clerk thereof; any person so obtaining a license shall pay to the Clerk the sum of twenty-five dollars for such license, and take an oath to support the Constitution, and abide by the laws of the Sac and Fox Nation, which oath may be administered by the Principal Chief, or the Clerk of the National Council authorized for that purpose, and it shall be the duty of the Clerk to record the same in the Journals of the National Council. But if any such white man or citizen of the United States, shall refuse to subscribe to the oath he shall not be entitled to the rights of citizenship, and shall forthwith be removed without the limits of the Sac and Fox Nation.

SEC. 27. All non-citizens being married to citizens of this Nation, or having children entitled to citizenship, shall have a right to live in this Nation and enjoy all the privileges enjoyed by other citizens, except participation in the annuities and final participation in the lands or funds realized by the Nation from the use of its lands, and in case of removal from the limits of our Nation, shall not have the right to sell their improvements, provided that such person shall satisfy the Principal Chief as to their good charcter and honest intentions, and provided that the principal Chief shall grant to such person permit to reside in the Nation during good behavior, with the consent of the National Council.

SEC. 28. The Principal Chief is hereby authorized to grant the permits herein provided for on the approval of the Executive Council.

SEC. 29. No non-citizen shall have a right to reside in or to own any kind of property within the Sac and Fox Nation except by permit, and any non-citizen, without a permit, who shall make any improvements in the Sac and Fox Nation, shall forfeit the same to the Nation.

SEC. 30. Non-citizens are all persons who are not of Sac and Fox blood, but this article shall not be construed so as to interfere with persons who are lawfully intermarried with citizens of the Sac and Fox Nation, or so as to interfere with any rights guaranteed by treaty. *Provided*, That this article shall not be so construed as to grant to citizens, not of Sac and Fox blood, to amass large herds of stock of any kind or to open up for cultivation large and numerous tracts of land, to the detriment of the citizens of the Sac and Fox Nation.

ARTICLE X.

Executions.

SEC. 31. The punishment of death in all cases shall be by hanging by the neck or shooting until he be dead, and the sentence shall at the time and place directed by the Judge, be executed by the high Sheriff, or some one deputized by him for that purpose.

ARTICLE XI.

Traders.

SEC. 32. All persons who carry on any business transactions within the limits of this Nation, under license from the United States Government, shall be required to pay the sum of one hundred and fifty dollars per annum into the National Treasury of this Nation, and it shall be the duty of the Treasurer of this Nation to collect the same.

SEC. 33. No non-citizen, licensed trader, who has not intermarried with a citizen of this Nation, shall be allowed to cut and put up hay from our common pasturage, or to cut or have cut firewood, poles, rails or logs from our forest without proper compensation, and under a permit from the Executive Council of the Sac and Fox Nation. *Provided,* That this article shall not be so constructed as to apply to Government employes or missionaries connected with the Indian service; and any non-citizen, licensed, found cutting and putting up hay from our common pasturage shall be fined ten dollars for each acre so cut and put up, and any non-citizen, licensed trader, found cutting or having cut from our forests, firewood, poles, rails, or logs, shall be fined the sum of twenty-five dollars for each and every offense.

SEC. 34. No non-citizen, licensed trader, shall be allowed to keep stock ranches nor cattle, horses or hogs within the limits of this Nation, except such horses as are actually necessary for use in connection with their business, and such milch cows as are actually necessary to furnish milk and butter for family use, and any licensed trader of this class, who shall disobey these provisions, shall be reported to the United States Agent, by the National Attorney, with the request that said person's license be revoked, and that they be removed from the limits of the Sac and Fox Nation.

ARTICLE XII.

Hotel Keepers.

SEC. 35. All non-citizens who may desire to operate a hotel, eating or boarding house of whatsoever kind, in the Sac and Fox Nation shall pay the same license and in the same manner, and be subject to the same restrictions as are non-citizen license traders.

SEC. 36. Every person transacting or proposing to transact a mercantile or hotel business in the Sac and Fox Nation, shall make application and receive license for that purpose from the Sac and Fox Executive Council, and before entering upon the business shall pay into the National Treasury the full sum of their license.

SEC. 37. It shall be and is hereby made the duty of the Sheriff where citizens of the United States violate the intent of this or any act regarding licensed traders or hotel keepers, to at once report the matter to the Indian Agent in charge or other officers of the U. S. and to request said officers to take proper action thereon.

ARTICLE XIII.

Indians not of Sac and Fox Blood.

SEC. 38. Any Indian residing in the Sac and Fox Nation, by virtue of marriage, permit, or otherwise, not of Sac and Fox blood, who shall advise with Council, or in any way interfere by conversation, act, or otherwise with the advancement of the Sac and Fox people, create any kind of dissatisfaction, contention or strife of any nature whatsoever, shall by the Prosecuting Attorney be reported to the Indian Agent and his removal from the Sac and Fox Nation demanded. *Provided,* However, that this section shall not be construed as to interfere with the U. S. interpreter or missionaries in the discharge of their respective duties.

ARTICLE XIV.

SEC. 39. All wild hogs in the Sac and Fox Nation are hereby declared to be the common property of the citizens of said Nation and any citizen who shall kill a wild hog in the Sac and Fox Nation, shall turn over to the National Treasury one-half of the value of each and every hog so killed, in cash, and upon the conviction of his failure to do so shall be fined in a sum equal to double the value thereof, or to receive not less than ten nor more than thirty lashes on the bare back for each and every offense, or both in the discretion of the court.

CHAPTER III.—ARTICLE I.

Relating to the Judiciary.

SEC. 40. The seat of the Sac and Fox government is hereby established at the Sac and Fox Agency.

SEC. 41. The court established under the government of this Nation shall have jurisdiction of all suits rising under the constitution and laws of the Sac and Fox Nation.

SEC. 42. There shall be established a Supreme Court which shall consist of one Chief Justice and two Associate Judges, who shall decide all civil cases.

SEC. 43. It shall be the duty of the three Judges to choose two persons of good character and knowledge, who shall in conjunction constitute a court for the purpose of hearing and deciding all criminal cases.

SEC. 44. No citizen of the Sac and Fox Nation who may be employed by the United States Government, as a police, shall be chosen to sit as judge in the court of the Sac and Fox Nation.

SEC. 45. The commencement of all suits shall be by summons obtained from the clerk of the court, and which summons shall state the nature of the case upon which proceedings are founded, and be served by some lawful officer at least twenty days before the holding of said court, except in criminal cases where witness can be immediately had, and such summons shall be returnable to the clerk with a certificate of service, and the court shall give judgment as to the right of the cause, and the matter in law shall appear under them without regarding any imperfection, defect or want of form in such summons in process.

SEC. 46. The court shall hold regular sessions on the first Mondays of May and November, but will convene in special term for the trial of any cause upon the order of the Executive Council.

ARTICLE II.

High Sheriff.

SEC. 47. The office of High Sheriff is hereby created. He shall be elected by the National Council for the term of two years.

SEC. 48. The Sheriff shall at all times keep the Council Room clean and properly ventilated, and during the session of the National Council or Executive Council and Court, well warmed and supplied with pure water. It shall be his especial duty to cause to be prosecuted every person who shall be accused of violating the laws.

SEC. 49. The High Sheriff shall be a conservator of the peace with such general powers as are exercised by Sheriffs, besides such special or extraordinary powers as may be conferred upon him by law. He shall wait upon, open and adjourn the sessions of the court and execute its mandates. He shall also wait upon and execute all orders of the National or Executive Council, who shall have full authority, during the session of the Council, and at all other times to suppress within the vicinity of the Council House all riotous broils, obscene, or other improper conduct, and to enforce obedience to the law and may, whenever necessary, summons any extra adequate force to his assistance; he may summarily arrest, imprison and hold until duly sober, any person acting improperly, while under the influence of intoxicating drinks, and arrest, and imprison all persons who may be guilty of a breach of the peace at or about the seat of government.

SEC. 50. The High Sheriff shall have the power to select one Under Sheriff from each treaty band to be approved by the Executive Council, and shall have general supervision over them and see that they properly execute all matters entrusted to them, and he shall see that all license fines, not otherwise provided for by law, are collected.

SEC. 51. The Under Sheriff shall be subject to the orders of the High Sheriff in the execution of the duties of his office under the same rules, regulations and restrictions as are imposed upon the High Sheriff by law.

SEC. 52. Should any person charged with criminal violation of the law resist any lawful officer, or person authorized to make arrest, while in the discharge of his or their duty, and such persons should be killed on account of unlawful resistance, such officer or other person shall not be held guilty of murder.

ARTICLE III.

Executive Council.

SEC. 53. The Executive Council shall consist of the number and serve for the length of time as defined by the constitution. They shall perform such duties as are required of them by the constitution, and such as are or may be required of them by law.

ARTICLE IV.

Prosecuting Attorney.

SEC. 54. The Prosecuting Attorney shall be elected by the National Council, and his term of office shall be that of the National Council electing him, and such Prosecuting Attorney before entering upon the duties of his office shall be commissioned by the Principal Chief.

SEC. 55. That it shall be the duty of the Prosecuting Attorney to prosecute in behalf of the Nation all persons charged with criminal offenses that may be brought before the court of the Nation, and be required to take the following oath or affirmation: "You do solemnly swear that you as prosecuting attorney for and on behalf of the Nation, will, to the best of your skill and ability, prosecute all persons charged with criminal offenses that may be brought before the court, and that you will not take or receive any remuneration of any person charged with any criminal offenses, but will be faithful to the Sac and Fox Nation in all prosecutions to the best of your ability, so help you God."

SEC. 56. There shall be a National Secretary, who shall be elected by the Council for the term of two years, who shall be clerk of the Council and court, and shall keep a record of all the proceedings of both the Council and court and perform such other duties that may be provided by law.

SEC. 57. There shall be a National Treasurer, who shall be elected by the Council for the term of two years; he shall give bond, with sureties, for the faithful preservation and disbursement of all funds which may come into his possession; the bond shall be in amount equal to double the amount of money likely to come into his possession, to be approved by the principal Chief, and to perform such other duties that may be provided by law.

ARTICLE V.

Attorneys.

SEC. 58. Before any citizen shall be allowed to appear before the court of this Nation for the purpose of practicing at law, he shall obtain a license from the clerk thereof, and pay in advance the sum of five dollars to practice before the court, and be required to take an oath that he will to the best of his knowledge and ability support and defend all cases that may be entrusted to his care.

SEC. 59. Before any non-citizen shall be allowed to appear before the court of this Nation for the purpose of practicing at law, he shall obtain a license from the clerk thereof, and pay in advance the sum of twenty dollars to practice before the court, and be required to take such an oath as is prescribed in the above section.

SEC. 60. Any persons engaged in the practice of law, agreeable to the provisions of this act, who shall be convicted before the court, of bribing or otherwise influencing any person to keep from appearing at court or proving unfaithful to their duties and oaths, shall be subject to a fine of twenty-five dollars, and the revocation of their license.

All fines collected under the provisions of this act shall be paid into the treasury.

SEC. 61. The Assistant Principal Chief shall be the presiding officer over the National Council.

SEC. 62. All the foregoing acts to take effect and be in force from and after their approval by the Principal Chief.

Approved April 6th, A. D. 1885

WITNESS:

I. A. TAYLOR. UCQUAW HO KO, his X mark,

E. N. GATSE. *Principal Chief.*

I certify that the foregoing is a correct copy of the Constitution and Laws adopted by the Sac and Fox Constitutional Convention and the Sac and Fox National Council.

CHAS. KEOKUK,

Sac and Fox Agency, I. T., April 6, 1885. *Secretary.*

ARTICLE I.

An Act for the Punishment of Criminal Offenses.

SEC. 3. Any person who is or may be convicted of threatening to kill another shall be adjudged to pay a fine of fifty dollars, and thirty days in jail, or more, or both, at the discretion of the Court.

Was read first, second and third time, and passed. Approved by me October 27, 1887.

MOSES KEOKUK, his X mark.

Principal Chief Sac and Fox Nation.

All Whipping Laws hereby repealed. Approved by me this 27th day of October, 1887.

MOSES KEOKUK, his X mark.

Principal Chief Sac and Fox Nation.

SEC. 4. That, upon trial and conviction of any person charged with the offense of having committed, or attempted to commit, a rape on any female, he shall be punished with not less than thirty days in jail, or more, at the discretion of the Court, or fifty dollars fine, or both.

Read first, second and third time, and passed.

MOSES KEOKUK, his X mark.

Principal Chief Sac and Fox Nation.

Whipping Laws hereby repealed. Approved by me this 27th day of October, 1887.

MOSES KEOKUK, his X mark.

Principal Chief Sac and Fox Nation.

ARTICLE II.

An Act for the Punishment of Theft.

SEC. 1. That any person who shall be convicted of stealing a horse, mule, jack or jennet, shall be punished by not less than one year imprisonment in the National Jail, and twenty-five dollars fine, to be paid into the National Treasury; and shall be compelled to make payment to the amount of damages or injuries sustained, if such stolen property be not restored, for the benefit of the person so injured, and for all other property, which shall be in proportion to the magnitude of the offense, at the discretion of the Court, and judgment against the offender for damages to the party injured.

Whipping Law herewith are hereby repealed. Read first, second and third time, and passed.

Oct. 28, 1887.

MOSES KEOKUK, his X mark.

Principal Chief Sac and Fox Nation.

SEC. 2. That if any person shall wilfully and maliciously burn the house or other property of another or (otherwise) kill any animal, or destroy the property of any person for the purpose of injury or of gratifying a spirit of revenge, or otherwise, shall be punished in like manner as provided in Section above, and be compelled to make ample remuneration by such compensation as the Court may determine.

Read first, second and third time, and passed.

Oct. 28, 1887.

MOSES KEOKUK, his X mark.

Principal Chief Sac and Fox Nation.

New Sec. Hereafter persons shall not be allowed to burn around the fields before the first day of May of each year for spring burn, and July first to August first of each year for late or summer burn, and October twenty-fifth to November first of each year.

Read first, second and third time, and passed.

October 28, 1887. MOSES KEOKUK, His X Mark.
Principal Chief Sac and Fox Nation

ARTICLE V.

Employment of Non-citizens.

Sec. 15. Any citizen of this Nation who shall hire or employ any citizen of the United States in any other manner than as provided in the first and second sections of this article, shall be deemed guilty of misdemeanor, and upon conviction be fined in any sum not less than twenty-five dollars and not exceeding fifty dollars at the discretion of the Court.

Sec. 19. Employers shall pay in advance for the person they hire.

Read first, second and third time, and passed.

Sec. 16, Art. 5 is hereby and herewith repealed.

MOSES KEOKUK, His X Mark,
Principal Chief Sac and Fox Nation.

Sec. 29. Changed to conform with the above Sec. 19.
October 1887.

ARTICLE VI.

Sec. 21 is hereby canceled.

MOSES KEOKUK, His X Mark.
October 28, 1887. *Principal Chief Sac and Fox Nation.*

Sec. 39 Art. 14, in regard to killing Wild Hogs is hereby repealed.
October 28, 1887. MOSES KEOKUK, His X Mark,
Principal Chief Sac and Fox Nation.

ARTICLE XI.

Sec. 8 is hereby repealed and instead the following is hereby enacted.

Sec. 8, Art. 11. Any person or persons being in a state of intoxication in Sac and Fox Agency, Indian Territory, shall upon conviction thereof before the court of this Nation be fined for each offense the sum of not less than twenty-five dollars and not more than fifty dollars, or one month imprisonment.

Passed and approved after third reading.

October 27, 1887. MOSES KEOKUK, His X Mark,
Principal Chief of Sac and Fox Nation.

New Sec. to come in Art. 11, after Sec. 8 of said Art. 11. Sheriff shall have power to arrest any non-citizen of Sac and Fox blood found in a state of intoxication within one mile of the Sac and Fox Agency,

Indian Territory, and bring the offender before the United States Indian Agent, and request his removal from the limits of Sac and Fox Nation.

Passed after third reading and approved by me, this 27th day of October, 1887.

MOSES KEOKUK, His X Mark.
Principal Chief, Sac and Fox Nation.

Resisting Officers.

SCE. 4, ART. 7.—Any person who shall resist, abuse or injure any officer of this Nation who is in the legal discharge of his duties shall, upon conviction, be punished for each offense not less than thirty days in the National jail, or not less than fifty dollars fine, or both.

Read first, second and third time, and passed.

MOSES KEOKUK, His X Mark.
October 28, 1887. *Principal Chief Sac and Fox Nation.*

NEW SEC. ART. 3.—That if any person or persons who shall be convicted for carrying deadly weapons within one mile of any public gathering, lawfully assembled, shall be punished by a fine of not less than five dollars nor more than ten dollars, at the discretion of the court.

Passed after third reading and approved by me, this 27th day of October, 1887. MOSES KEOKUK, His X Mark,
Principal Chief Sac and Fox Nation.

Sheriff.

NEW SEC.—Sheriff may take possession of property in dispute and return the same to the proper owner when commanded to do so by the Secretary of the Nation. *Provided*, said Secretary of the Nation is in possession of sufficient evidence and circumstances produced by plaintiffs or others to justify said Secretary to issue said command, with the approval of the Principal Chief; *provided, also*, the right of action still rests with the party or parties dispossessed of said property. This act to be in force and operative immediately after its passage.

Read first, second and third time, and passed.

MOSES KEOKUK, His X Mark,
Principal Chief Sac and Fox Nation.

Employment of non-citizens is amended. No taxes for laborers of Indian blood.

Passed after third reading.

Approved by me, this 24th day of October, 1887.

MOSES KEOKUK, His X Mark,
Principal Chief Sac and Fox Nation.

October 28, 1887.

NEW SEC. All small offences hereafter shall be tried before the National Secretary, who is hereby authorized to try and decide the same.

Read first, second and third time, and passed.

MOSES KEOKUK, His X Mark,
Principal Chief Sac and Fox Nation.

October 28, 1887.

SEC. 2, CHAP. 2, ART. 1.—The Whipping Law in this (Sec. 2, Art. I) is hereby repealed, and the fine the same.

Read first, second and third time, and passed.

MOSES KEOKUK, His X Mark,
Principal Chief Sac and Fox Nation.

EXTRACTS OF TREATY

Between the United States of America and the tribe of Sac and Fox Indians, of the Mississippi, of Oct. 14, 1863, and yet unfulfilled, alluded to in the foregoing Constitution and Laws:

* * * * * * * *

ARTICLE VI.

The United States agree, in consideration of the improvements upon the said reservation, to give to the Sacs and Foxes for their future home a tract of land in the Indian country south of Kansas, and south of the Cherokee lands, not exceeding seven hundred and fifty square miles in extent. The selection of such new reservation shall be made under the direction of the Secretary of the Interior, and with his approval, by commissioners appointed by the said Secretary, who shall visit the Indian country, with delegations from all tribes proposing to remove thereto, as soon as practicable after the ratification of this treaty; and said reservation shall be surveyed as to its exterior lines, at the cost of the United States, under the direction of the Commissioner of Indian Affairs, not to exceed three thousand dollars: *Provided*, That if it shall be found impracticable to select a suitable home for the tribe except by purchase from the Cherokees, the United States will pay toward the said purchase the same amount that would have been payable to the Creeks if the reservation had been selected upon the former Creek lands; and in that case the balance of money payable to the Cherokees shall be deducted from the amount due the Sacs and Foxes under this treaty.

ARTICLE VII.

As soon as practicable after the selection of the new reservation herein provided for, there shall be erected thereon, at the cost of the United States, a dwelling-house for the agent of the tribe, a house and shop for a blacksmith, and dwelling-house for a physician, the aggregate cost of which shall not exceed ten thousand dollars; and also, at the expense of the tribe, five dwelling-houses for the chiefs, to cost in all not more than five thousand dollars.

* * * * * * * *

ARTICLE VIII.

No part of the invested funds of the tribe, or of any moneys which may be due to them under the provisions of previous treaties, nor of any moneys provided to be paid to them by this treaty, shall be used in payment of any claims against the tribe accruing previous to the ratification of this treaty, unless herein expressly provided for.

ARTICLE IX.

In order to promote the civilization of the tribe, one section of land, convenient to the residence of the agent, shall be selected by said agent, with the approval of the Commissioner of Indian Affairs, and set apart for a manual-labor school; and there shall also be set apart, from the money to be paid to the tribe under this treaty, the sum of ten thousand dollars for the erection of the necessary school buildings and dwelling for teacher, and the annual amount of five thousand dollars shall be set apart from the income of their funds after the erection of such school buildings, for the support of the school; and after the settlement of the tribe upon their new reservation, the sum of five thousand dollars of the income of their funds may be annually used, under the direction of the chiefs, in the support of their national government, out of which last mentioned amount the sum of five hundred dollars shall be annually paid to each of the chiefs.

* * * * * * * *

ARTICLE XIV.

The Sacs and Foxes, parties to this treaty, agree that the Sacs and Foxes of Missouri, if they shall so elect, with the approval of the Secretary of the Interior, may unite with them and become a part of their people, upon their contributing to the common fund such a portion of their funds as will place them on equal footing in regard to annuities.

ARTICLE XV.

The claims of the Sacs and Foxes against the United States for stealing of stock, which have heretofore been adjusted, amounting to sixteen thousand four hundred dollars, shall be paid by the United States, and the amount disbursed and expended for the benefit of the tribe in such objects for their improvement and comfort upon the new reservation, as the chiefs through their agent shall desire; and whereas the Indians claim that one full payment due under previous treaty has never been made to them, it is agreed that a careful examination of the books of the Commissioner of Indian Affairs shall be made, and if any sum is found to be still due and unpaid, the same shall be paid to them per capita, in the same manner as their annuities are paid.

* * * * * * * *

ARTICLE XXI.

The Sacs and Foxes of the Mississippi, parties to this agreement, being anxious that all the members of their tribe shall participate in the advantages to be derived from the investment of their national funds, sales of lands, and so forth, it is therefore agreed that, as soon as practicable, the Commissioner of Indian Affairs shall cause the necessary proceedings to be adopted to have such members of the tribe as may be absent notified of this agreement and its advantages, and to induce them to come in and permanently unite with their brethren; and that no part of the funds arising from or due the Nation under this or previous treaty stipulations, shall be paid to any bands or parts of bands who do not permanently reside on the reservation set apart to them by the Government in the Indian Territory, as provided in this treaty, except those residing in the State of Iowa; and it is further agreed, that all money accruing from this or former treaties, now due or to become due said Nation, shall be paid them on their reservation in Kansas; and after their removal, as provided in this treaty, payments shall be made at their agency on their lands as then located.

DEPARTMENT OF THE INTERIOR,
WASHINGTON, April 19, 1887.

Moses Keokuk, Head Chief Sac and Fox Tribe of Indians:

SIR—In regard to your suggestion that the Chiefs of your tribe be allowed to examine and report any irregularities in the management of the school, the Commissioner says that his office will "be glad to have them examine and report at any time, and any suggestions or recommendations made by them will receive prompt attention."

Of course your visits to the school must be subject to such regulations as to time, etc., as the Agent may prescribe, so as not to interfere with proper discipline.

Very respectfully,

H. L. MULDROW,

Acting Secretary.

DEPARTMENT OF THE INTERIOR,
WASHINGTON, Feb. 12, 1887.

The Commissioner of Indian Affairs:

SIR—The department is in receipt of your letter of January 3, 1887, with enclosures on the subject of the proper action to be taken regarding certaiu funds due to the Sac and Fox Indians, under treaty of February 18, 1867 (15 Stat., 495), and requesting to be instructed on the following points.

1st. "Should Mokohoko's band be allowed to elect a Chief to fill Mokohoko's place in the Sac and Fox National Government, and to be paid $500 per annum from the money in question?"

2d. Does the clause in the treaty above referred to, which reads * * * out of which last mentioned amount the sum of $500 shall be annually paid to each of the chiefs entitle the chief of the band in Iowa to such payment, in view of article 21 of same treaty?"

3d. "Shall the balance of this fund, $5,000, which may be left each year after payment of the chiefs, be turned over to the National Treasurer, * * * or be held by the Agent and used by him under direction of the chiefs in support of the National Government?"

The 9th article of the treaty, as originally agreed upon, provides that "the sum of five hundred dollars shall be annually paid to each of the five chiefs," etc. But as amended by the Senate and finally adopted and ratified, the clause bearing particularly upon the first question, reads as follows:

"And after settlement of the tribe upon their new reservation the sum of five thousand dollars of the income of their funds may be annually used under the directions of the chiefs, in the support of their National Government, out of which last mentioned amount the sum of five hundred dollars shall be annually paid to each of the chiefs."

The treaty therefore does not specify the number of chiefs to whom the payment shall be made. It is the policy of the Government to encourage the gradual abolition of the tribal system and to promote among the Indians such measures as will facilitate the incorporation of the race into our political and social system as citizens.

The present Agent of these Indians, in a reply of December 23, 1886, to your office on this subject, says:

"Relative to recognizing a salried Chief from the Mokohoko band, I do not think it advisable for this reason: Should they be allowed a chief, would select 'Pahshepawho.' A person more unsuitable could not be found in America, for he is stubborn, lazy and exceedingly dull, and besides, I do not believe in adding to the number of chiefs at present. But the band should have voice in the National Council just as soon as they request it."

The Department need not enter in the consideration at this time of the question whether there shall be four or whether there shall be five chiefs of the tribe, or whether this band or the other band shall be entitled to a salaried chief; its main duty in the premises is to ascertain who *are* the chiefs recognized as such by the tribe, and to pay annually to each of the recognized chiefs of the tribe settled on the new reservation in the Indian Territory, the sum of five hundred dollars, as specified in the treaty.

The foregoing answers also the second of the series of above questions propounded by you. The point raised in that question, however, was fully covered by Department letter of June 1, 1886, from which the following quotation is made:

"To what extent then are the Sacs and Foxes living in the State of Iowa excepted from the obligations of the treaty? Simply this: Their right to remain in Iowa is recognized without forfeiting their right to share in the common fund. No band or parts of bands who do not reside on the reservation shall be paid any part of said fund, except those living in the State of Iowa. This is the sole exception in their favor; but they are equally bound by the treaty stipulation providing that from the common fund shall be deducted the amounts specified for the support of the school and the National Government. If it was not intended that the sum so provided to be set apart annually from the income of their funds should be deducted from the common fund before distribution, why not have said that there shall be apportioned among the Sacs and Foxes of Mississippi their proportion of the amount appropriated by this act, and from the amount so apportioned and due to the Sacs and Foxes living on the reservation there shall be set apart the sum of $5,000 for the support of the school, and $5,000 for the support of the Government? But if there is any question as to the construction of this treaty, in reference to the proper disposition of this fund, the act of 1885 (23 Stat. 373) making appropriation for the Sacs and Foxes of the Mississippi, removes all doubt. That act appropriates $51,000 for the said Indians, and provides that the sum of $1.500 shall be used for pay of a physician and medicine for the use of said Indians. It also provides that "hereafter the Sacs and Foxes of Iowa shall have apportioned to them from appropriations for fulfilling the stipulations of said treaties, their per capita proportion of the amount appropriated in this act, subject to provisions of treaties with said tribes, * * * that this shall apply only to the (original) Sacs and Foxes now in Iowa. * * *."

What are the provisions, of the treaty to which their apportionment is subject? Clearly, the specific charge of $10,000 which by the treaty was provided to be *set apart from the income of their funds*. A careful examination of the treaty fails to show that the income to be paid annually to these Indians is subject to any other provision. I think it therefore plain, that the sum of $10,000 should be deducted from the $51,000 appropriated, before the per capita distribution is made to the several bands."

Considering now the third question, the Agent reports that the National Treasurer "is a young man of fair education, good business qualifications, and in every manner fully competent to perform the duties of the office." He is under six thousand ($6,000) dollars bond, and the Agent thinks the balance of the fund ($3,000) for the National Government of the tribe, left after making the payments to the chiefs, should be turned over to him.

Moses Keokuk, the Principal Chief, asks in a telegram which accompanies the papers, that the Agent be instructed "to turn our National funds over to our Treasurer."

The tribe has adopted a Constitution, which is with the papers, and have organized a National Government thereunder.

In Section 1, Article 2 of the Constitution, it is provided that "the powers of this Government shall be divided into three distinct departments, the Legislative, the Executive and the Judicial." In Article 4 provision is made in Sections 18 to 22, inclusive, for the choosing of a Treasurer by the National Council for the term of two years, prescribing the bond for the faithful discharge of his trust, the manner in which money shall be drawn from the Treasury, which is required to be by warrant from the Principal Chief, and in consequence of appropriations made by law; also prescribing the manner of accountability for receipts and expenditures, and specifying the time which shall constitute the fiscal year of the Nation.

The money which the tribe desires shall be turned over to their National Treasurer is dedicated by the treaty "to be annually used under the direction of the chiefs in support of their National Government." The treaty seems to contemplate just what the tribe desire and request may be done.

Though there may be misgivings that the money may not be used for and applied to proper and legitimate objects and purposes, the tribe should be encouraged after having proceeded so far in the inauguration of their National Government provided for under the treaty, to take all proper steps necessary to put it into full operation.

It cannot be reasonably expected that they will learn and exercise the principles and measures of self-government that regulate civilized communities, unless they are permitted to assume the duties and responsibilities which necessarily lead thereto.

No more can it be expected that the conduct of their National affairs will not be attended, to some extent, with failures and consequent embarrassments; but experience will no doubt guide them into better methods of management of their government.

The money will therefore, for this time at least, be paid over to the National Treasurer of the tribe as requested.

Very respectfully,

L. Q. C. LAMAR,

Secretary.